eckie Leckie
tland's leading educational publishers



# National 5
# ADMINISTRATION & IT
## *COURSE NOTES*

N5 ADMINISTRATION & IT *COURSE NOTES*



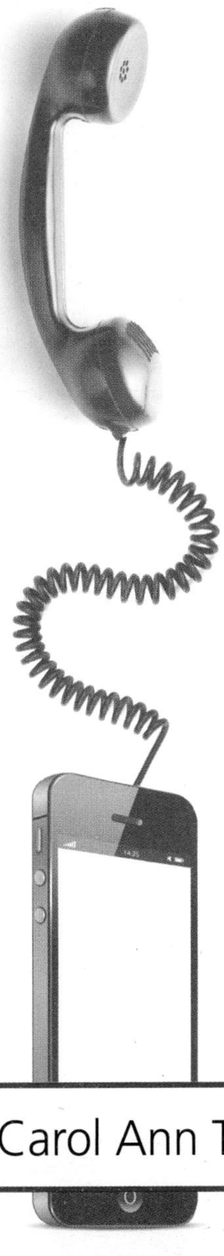

Kathryn Pearce • Carol Ann Taylor

001/27052013

10 9 8 7 6 5 4 3



ISBN 9780007504756

*Published by*
Leckie & Leckie Ltd
An imprint of HarperCollins*Publishers*
Westerhill Road, Bishopbriggs, Glasgow, G64 2QT
T: 0844 576 8126 F: 0844 576 8131
leckieandleckie@harpercollins.co.uk www.leckieandleckie.co.uk

*Special thanks to*
Donna Cole (copyediting and proofreading)
Delphine Lawrance (picture research)
Eilidh Proudfoot (content review)

A CIP Catalogue record for this book is available from the British Library.

*Acknowledgements*
We would like to thank the following for permission to reproduce their material:
page 2-3 photo © David Pirvu; page 12-13 photo © Creativemarc; page 17 photo © NAN728; page 25 photo © Brian A Jackson; page 36 photo © auremar; page 36 photo © konstantynov; page 36 photo © sixninepixels; page 36 photo © Martin Novak; page 37 photo © tristan tan; page 42 photo © Creativemarc; page 54 photo © Monkey Business Images; page 55 photo © Odua Images; page 62-63 photo © Denys Prykhodov; page 85 photo © lucadp; page 91-95 Microsoft Excel spreadsheet excerpts used with permission from Microsoft; page 114-115 photo © Hasloo Group Production Studio; page 116 Microsoft Word ribbon screenshot used with permission from Microsoft; page 120 photo © sheelamohanachandran2010; page 132 Microsoft PowerPoint graphic used with permission from Microsoft; page 132 Microsoft PowerPoint slide template used with permission from Microsoft; page 133 Microsoft PowerPoint slides used with permission from Microsoft; page 134 Microsoft PowerPoint graphics used with permission from Microsoft; page 135 Microsoft PowerPoint graphics used with permission from Microsoft; page 136 Microsoft PowerPoint slide templates used with permission from Microsoft; page 137 Microsoft PowerPoint slides used with permission from Microsoft; page 143 Microsoft Publisher graphic used with permission from Microsoft; page 144 Microsoft Publisher templates used with permission from Microsoft; page 145 Microsoft Publisher templates used with permission from Microsoft; page 150 Microsoft Outlook screenshot used with permission from Microsoft; page 152 photo © Maksim Shmeljov; page 153 photo © Cienpies Design

Whilst every effort has been made to trace the copyright holders, in cases where this has been unsuccessful, or if any have inadvertently been overlooked, the Publishers would gladly receive any information enabling them to rectify any error or omission at the first opportunity.

*About the authors*
Carol Ann Taylor is a Business Education teacher at Duncanrig Secondary School in East Kilbride. She has been a setter and Principal Assessor for Standard Grade Administration and is currently working with the SQA on National 5 Administration & IT.

Kathryn Pearce has been teaching in Our Lady & St Patrick's High in Dumbarton since 1995. She has been a setter and examiner for Standard Grade Administration since 2001 and is currently working with the SQA on National 5 Administration & IT.

## Introduction



## UNIT 1 – Administrative Practices



## UNIT 2 – IT Solutions for Administrators



## UNIT 3 – Communication in Administration



## Answers

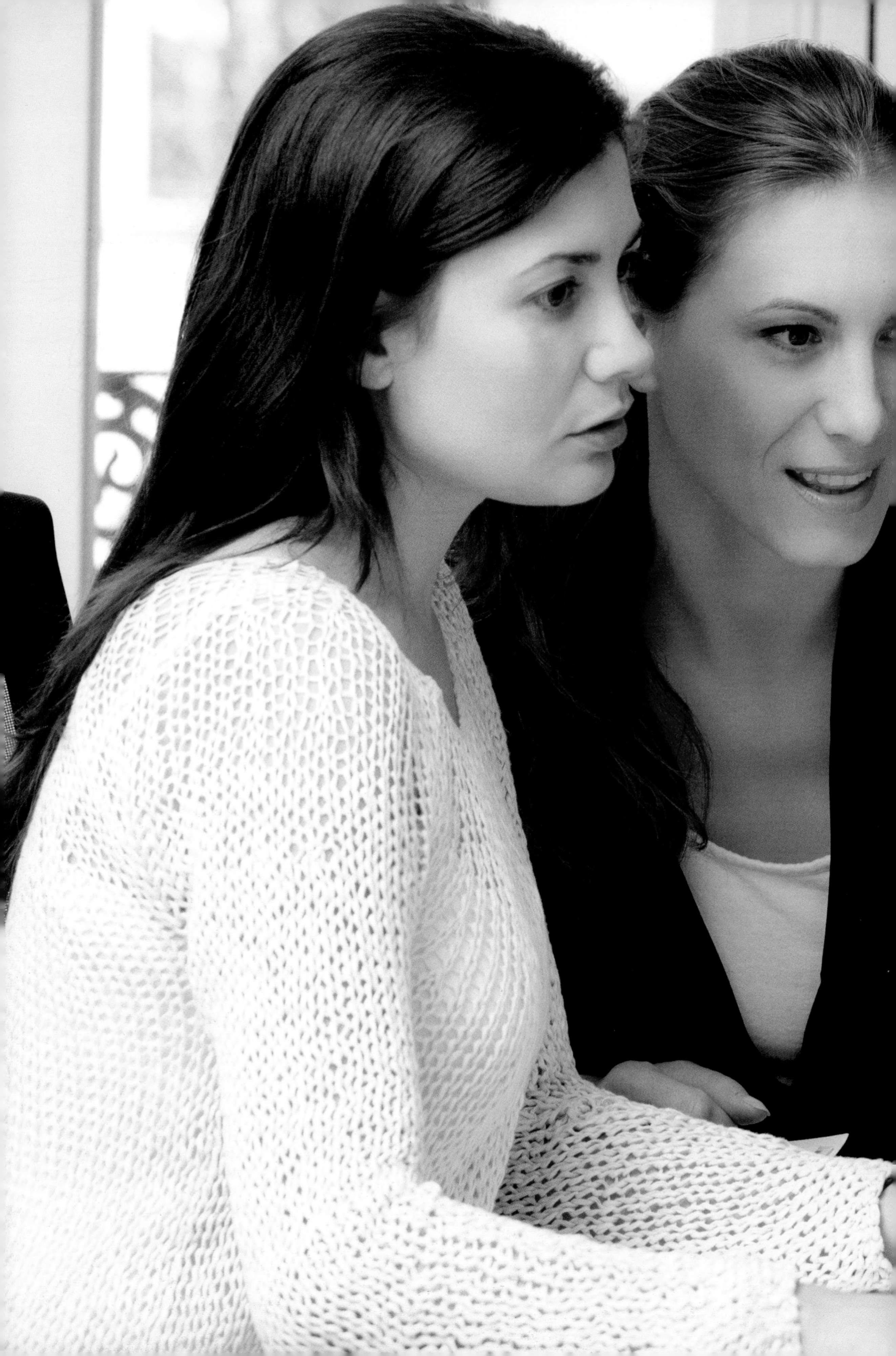

# Administration and IT

# About this book

## You will also find the following sections in this book:

- **You should already know** – previous knowledge that you should have gained from Level 3 and Level 4 Outcomes and Experiences, which will help you with the chapter.
- **Learning intentions** – an indication of what you are expected to learn in this chapter.
- **Watch points** – these provide suggestions to help complete tasks successfully.
- **Make the link** – examples of how you can use your administration and IT skills in a number of different subjects.
- **Skills** – skills that the chapter helps you to develop.
- **Questions** – to test your knowledge and understanding of the course. Practical tasks test your IT skills.
- **Key question** – if you can complete this question it demonstrates that you have reached the required standard.
- **Learning checklist** – to help you determine which parts of the chapter you are confident with and which parts you may need to revise further. All the learning checklists are available to download from the Leckie & Leckie website.
- **National 5** – Any sections which are shaded like this one are for National 5 only.

### Integrative Course

In this course there will be an emphasis on skills development and the application of those skills. The course contains a significant practical element, which encourages the integration of skills, knowledge and understanding through practical activities.

While the skills, knowledge and understanding covered in this book help to develop and reflect current administrative practice, the course is flexible to take account of new technologies as they develop.

### Software

This book is designed to be generic in nature and therefore does not contain step-by-step instructions for the use of specific software.

## Resources to Download

For many of the activities in this book you can download resources from the Leckie & Leckie website. To access these materials go to the page for this book on the Leckie & Leckie website (http://ow.ly/lcHkz) and select the 'Online Resources' tab. You will also find all the Learning Checklists here.

# Introduction

## Why choose Administration and IT?

Administration supports the effective running of organisations across the economy, and offers wide-ranging employment opportunities. This course makes an important contribution to general education through developing a range of essential skills that will stand you in good stead regardless of the career path you eventually choose. It is also extremely useful in other walks of life. For example being organised and being able to produce professional-looking documents could be extremely useful for producing coursework at college/university.

This course will develop your administrative and IT skills and will allow you to contribute to the effective working of an organisation.

### The course

To pass the course at National 4 level you must pass all three of the units, as well as the Added Value Unit. These are all marked by your teacher. The Added Value Unit takes the form of an assignment, and its purpose is to draw on the knowledge, understanding and skills developed in the other three units. You will undertake practical administration- and IT-based tasks to organise and support a small-scale event or events.

To pass the course at National 5 level you must pass all three of the units that are marked by your teacher. You will also sit an Assignment, which is marked by an SQA marker. You will be awarded a grade at National 5 based on your mark in the Assignment.

The three units studied at both National 4 and National 5 levels are:

- Administrative Practices
  The purpose of this unit is to give you a basic introduction to administration in the workplace. You will begin to appreciate important legislation affecting employees, key features of good customer care, and the skills, qualities and attributes required of administrators. The unit will also allow you to apply this basic understanding to carry out a range of straightforward administrative tasks required for organising and supporting small-scale events.

- IT Solutions for Administrators
  The purpose of this unit is to develop your basic skills in IT and organising and processing simple information in familiar administration-related contexts. You will use the following IT

applications: word processing, spreadsheets and databases to create and edit simple business documents. The unit will allow emerging technologies to be incorporated in order to ensure that its content remains current and relevant.

- Communication in Administration
  The purpose of this unit is to allow you to use IT for gathering and sharing simple information with others in familiar administration-related contexts. You will develop a basic understanding of what constitutes a reliable source of information and an ability to use appropriate methods for gathering information. You will also become able to communicate simple information in ways that show a basic awareness of its context, audience and purpose. The unit will allow emerging technologies to be incorporated in order to ensure that its content remains current and relevant.

## Outcomes and assessment standards

| National 4<br>Administrative Practices<br>Outcome 1 | National 5 |
|---|---|
| Provide an overview of administration in the workplace by:<br>1. Naming the main tasks, skills and qualities of an administrative assistant.<br>2. Outlining the key features of good customer care.<br>3. Outlining the key employee responsibilities in terms of health and safety.<br>4. Outlining the key employee responsibilities in terms of the security of people, property and information. | Provide an account of administration in the workplace by:<br>1. Describing the tasks, skills and qualities of an administrative assistant.<br>2. Describing key features of good customer care in the context of administration.<br>3. Describing the organisational responsibilities in terms of health and safety.<br>4. Describing the key organisational responsibilities in terms of the security of people, property and information. |
| **Outcome 2** | |
| Carry out administrative tasks in the context of organising and supporting small-scale events, according to a simple brief by:<br>1. Carrying out straightforward planning tasks for the event.<br>2. Editing documents to support the event.<br>3. Carrying out follow-up activities. | Interpret a given brief and carry out administrative tasks in the context of organising and supporting events by:<br>1. Carrying out planning tasks, taking account of the budget available.<br>2. Preparing documents to support the event.<br>3. Carrying out follow-up activities. |

| IT Solutions for Adminstrators<br>Outcome 1 | |
|---|---|
| Use functions of a spreadsheet in line with a given task by:<br>1. Editing a spreadsheet, applying simple formulae.<br>2. Sorting data within the worksheet.<br>3. Creating a simple chart from a specified range. | Use a spreadsheet application, to interpret a given brief by:<br>1. Creating, editing and applying advanced functions and formulae to a workbook.<br>2. Creating a suitable chart. |

| Outcome 2 | |
|---|---|
| Use functions of a flat database in line with a given task by:<br>**1.** Populating a database, using forms.<br>**2.** Editing a database.<br>**3.** Manipulating information by searching and sorting.<br>**4.** Creating a simple report. | Use advanced functions of a relational database to interpret a given brief by:<br>**1.** Populating a database, using forms.<br>**2.** Editing a database.<br>**3.** Manipulating information in a simple relational database.<br>**4.** Presenting information in a report, to a professional standard. |
| **Outcome 3** | |
| Use functions of word processing in line with a given task by:<br>**1.** Creating and editing simple business documents, complying with the prescribed house style.<br>**2.** Creating a simple table and sorting the data.<br>**3.** Importing data into a simple business document. | Use advanced functions of word processing to interpret a given brief by:<br>**1.** Editing business documents, applying the house style.<br>**2.** Creating and/or editing a table.<br>**3.** Importing data from a spreadsheet and/ or database dynamically into a business document.<br>**4.** Merging appropriate data from a spreadsheet or database into a business document. |

| Communication in Administration<br>Outcome 1 | |
|---|---|
| Use technology to gather information in line with a simple brief by:<br>**1.** Searching for and extracting simple information from the Internet.<br>**2.** Searching for and extracting simple information using an internal network (intranet). | Use technology to extract information and be able to evaluate sources of information by:<br>**1.** Searching for and extracting/downloading relevant information to interpret a given brief.<br>**2.** Outlining key features of reliable sources of information.<br>**3.** Explaining the consequences of using unreliable Internet sources of information. |
| **Outcome 2** | |
| Use functions of technology to prepare and communicate simple information in line with a simple brief by:<br>**1.** Using multimedia to create a simple presentation.<br>**2.** Using desktop publishing to produce a simple document.<br>**3.** Using an electronic method to communicate information. | Use advanced functions of technology to prepare and communicate information by interpreting a given brief, to convey a professional image by:<br>**1.** Using functions of multimedia applications to create a presentation.<br>**2.** Using functions of desktop publishing to produce a document.<br>**3.** Using electronic methods to communicate information. |

**National 4**
**Added Value Assignment**
**Outcome 1**

The assignment will be carried out in class under supervision. This will be set and marked internally. Organise and support a small-scale event to a given brief, making use of current or emerging equivalent technologies, by:

1. Preparing for a small-scale event, making use of appropriate technologies where appropriate.
2. Preparing simple documents to support the event, using standard templates and utilising functions of IT applications.
3. Communicating using electronic methods, showing a basic awareness of the communication's context, audience and purpose.
4. Carrying out straightforward follow-up tasks, making use of appropriate technologies where necessary.

**National 5**
**Assignment**

The assignment will have 100 marks and will be carried out in class under exam conditions. This will be marked externally.

Stage 1: preparing for the event including contingency planning:

- Preparing a to-do list/priorities list.
- Entering details into an e-diary.
- Searching for information about the venue and resources and how to book them.
- Using spreadsheets to access relevant statistical or financial information, including the budget for the event.
- Using appropriate software to prepare the agenda.
- Using appropriate software to prepare materials, which could include name badges, advertising, invitations, place cards.
- Using databases for details of delegates/performers and to carry out the following functions: update, search, mail merge and prepare letters, labels, attendees' report.
- Using presentation software to prepare the key speaker's presentation, background/welcoming presentation.
- Resolve a double-booking of the venue.
- Prepare additional documents at short notice.
- Changing travel or other arrangements due to unforeseen circumstances.

Stage 2: follow-up tasks:

- Prepare an evaluation of the event.
- Collate responses and present findings in a variety of formats, including charts.
- Prepare 'thank you' letters (to the venue host, participants and guests), using mail merge.
- Prepare minutes, notes or action points.
- Prepare event costings and expenses.
- Administrative theory will be integrated within the tasks and will be awarded 10–20% of the mark.

## Other skills

Throughout all three units you will also develop skills in the areas shown below:

- **Numeracy**
  - Information handling
- **Employability, enterprise and citizenship**
  - Employability
  - Information and communication technology (ICT)

- **Thinking skills**
    - Remembering
    - Understanding
    - Applying

## Course progression

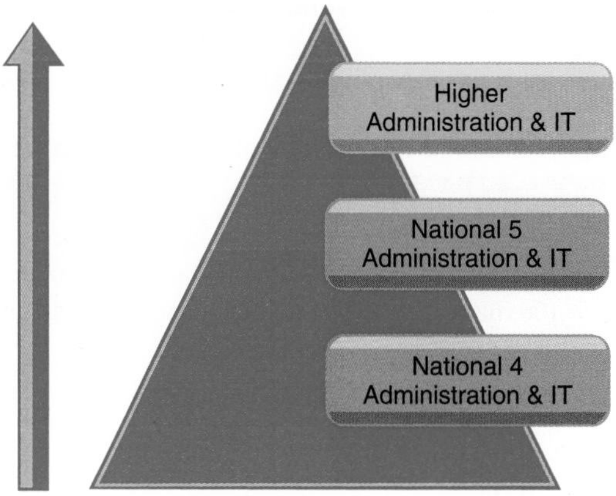

# 1

# Administrative Practices

# 1 Tasks, skills and qualities of an administrative assistant

**You should already know**

- By researching the organisation of a business, I can discuss the role of departments and personnel, evaluating how they contribute to the success or failure of the business. **SOC 4-22a**

**In this chapter you will learn about:**

- The tasks undertaken by an **admin assistant**.
- The skills and qualities required and/or possessed by an admin assistant.

## Tasks undertaken by an admin assistant

Administration helps any organisation run efficiently and in an organised way. The role of an admin assistant is therefore very important. An admin assistant will be required to fulfil a range of general administrative duties, such as receiving and sending e-mail, answering telephone enquiries, maintaining records, and so on. The range of tasks will depend on the size and type of organisation. For example, in a small organisation the admin assistant may be required to 'cover' reception, distribute mail, etc., whereas a large organisation will have specialist staff and departments to carry out these tasks.

The following diagram illustrates some of the tasks that may be expected of an administrative assistant.

**Watch point**

A task is a duty undertaken by the admin assistant.

Duties will be found in the job description.

## Skills and qualities

A skill is the ability to do something well, either through practising it or by gaining knowledge in the skill, for example IT. An admin assistant may have gained skills in **customer care** or **customer service**, meaning that they know how to treat customers well. Other skills include literacy skills, numeracy skills, communication skills, IT skills, etc.

A quality describes the type of person the job applicant is, for example:

- if they are organised
- if they can use their own initiative
- if they are dependable and reliable
- if they are patient, calm and tactful

## Finding the right person for the job

When an organisation is looking to appoint a new member of staff, they will draw up a **job description** and a **person specification**.

## Job description

Details relating to a specific job are usually found in a job description. This sets out some background to the post, the duties and tasks associated with the post, the post holder's responsibilities and who their line manager is. It will also provide information on the hours to be worked, the salary to be paid and the holiday entitlement.

A job applicant uses this document to decide if the job is right for them.

## Person specification

From the job description, the organisation can prepare a person specification. The roles and responsibilities detailed in the job description will highlight the skills, qualifications, experience and personal qualities required from a suitable candidate.

Each component of the person specification is usually classed as essential (a must-have skill or quality) or desirable (having this skill or quality would be an advantage, but it is not vital). Thus, a profile of the ideal candidate can be prepared and used to assist in the selection process.

> **Watch point**
> Qualities/skills will be found in the person specification.

A job applicant uses this document to decide if they have the necessary skills, qualifications, experience and personal qualities to be able to apply for the job.

A sample person specification for an admin assistant is shown below.

**Admin assistant – person specification**

| | Essential | Desirable |
|---|---|---|
| Skills, knowledge and abilities | • Ability to accurately key in data.<br>• Ability to create and edit word-processed documents.<br>• Ability to create and edit spreadsheets.<br>• Confidence at using e-mail and the Internet.<br>• Ability to file accurately.<br>• Ability to organise small-scale events. | • Ability to create and edit databases.<br>• Knowledge of prioritising workloads in order to meet deadlines.<br>• Ability to learn new ICT skills quickly. |
| Qualifications | • National 4/5 Administration and IT | • National 5 English and Maths |
| Experience | | • Previous administrative experience at a junior level. |
| Personal qualities | • Ability to quickly follow verbal and written instructions.<br>• Motivated and keen to learn.<br>• Can use own initiative or work as part of a team.<br>• Dependable/reliable. | • Organised.<br>• Good at time management. |

## What next?

Once a job applicant has decided that the job would suit them (based on the information provided in the job description) and that they have the necessary skills, experience and qualities (as identified in the person specification), they should apply for the job. This can be done in one of two ways:

- completing an application form
- drawing up a curriculum vitae (CV)

**Application forms** allow job applicants to provide information in a standardised format. Job applicants complete the form, giving full information about themselves, outlining their knowledge, skills and experience that are specifically identified in the job description and person specification.

A **CV** allows a job applicant to provide information about themselves in a format that they have created. Each job applicant's CV may contain different information.

The Human Resources (HR) department can then match each completed application form or CV with the job description and person specification to check the applicant's suitability for the job.

This will allow the organisation to draw up a short-list of suitable applicants for the job. These applicants will then be invited to attend for an interview, where the 'best person for the job' will be selected, and a job offer made.

Job applicants may be asked to enclose a reference (written statement from a referee) about their suitability for the job, or their references may be followed-up later.

The successful job applicant will be issued with a contract of employment (giving details of the job title, salary and working conditions) before they have started work.

**Watch point**

You must know the difference between an essential skill/ quality and a desirable skill/ quality.

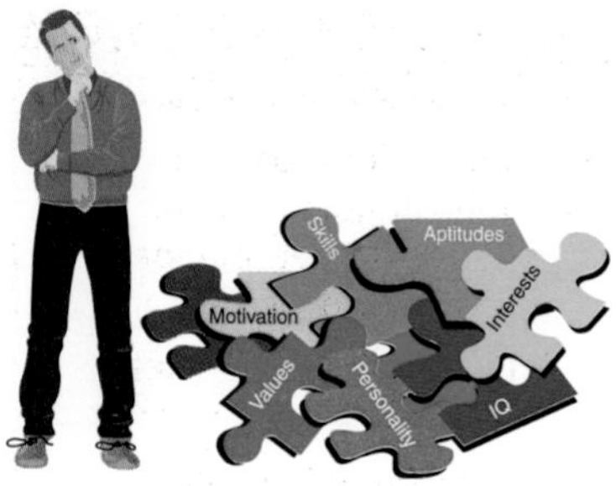


## Identifying current skills and gaps in skills

Most people find it difficult to assess their own skills and qualities. However, it is an important task that will highlight any areas you need to gain knowledge or experience in.

Staff development is vital to ensure that you are doing your job to the best of your ability. Training and development will also help further your career and may lead to a promotion in your organisation.

## Skill scan

A skill scan is a statement describing an individual's skills, knowledge and qualities to date. For example, consider the skills in the table below. For each, a rating of 1–4 is used where 1 indicates that the individual is very good at this skill and 4 indicates that the individual has no knowledge or experience of this skill.

| | Very good 1 | 2 | 3 | No knowledge 4 |
|---|---|---|---|---|
| Ability to prioritise workloads in order to meet deadlines. | | | | |
| Excellent verbal and written communication skills. | | | | |
| Excellent organisation and communication skills. | | | | |
| Awareness of health and safety issues. | | | | |
| Ability to deal with ICT equipment effectively. | | | | |
| Confident at using e-mail and the Internet. | | | | |
| Ability to use initiative and work unsupervised. | | | | |
| Ability to work as part of a team. | | | | |
| Ability to organise small-scale events. | | | | |

Having completed a skill scan, the individual will be able to analyse their own level of skill and knowledge. Columns 3 and 4 will highlight areas in which the individual needs further training and development.

An alternative approach to a skill scan may be to prepare a SWOT analysis, where an individual identifies their areas of strengths and weaknesses plus any opportunities and threats that they may face.

Skills, knowledge and qualities that require improvement will be highlighted under weaknesses and threats.

| Strengths | Weaknesses |
|---|---|
| – What positive characteristics does the individual have?<br>– What is the individual good at?<br>– Do other people compliment the individual on certain skills or qualities? | – Are there things that the individual does badly?<br>– What skills and abilities need improvement? |
| **Opportunities** | **Threats** |
| – What are the promising prospects facing the individual?<br>– Is the individual doing all that they can to ensure success in their studies and secure a job in the future?<br>– What more could they be doing? | – How are things likely to change in the future, especially with regard to IT?<br>– Will the individual be able to adapt?<br>– Are there any obstacles that could threaten their success on this course? |

## Make the link

- In the IT Solutions for Administrators unit you will use spreadsheet, database and word processing applications, or emerging equivalent technologies.
- In the Communication in Administration unit you will search, extract and download information, and use technology to prepare and communicate information.

## Activity

Watch the following video clip, which outlines the daily duties of an admin assistant and answer the questions that follow:
http://www.youtube.com/watch?v=NGmxgQzwZ-8

1. How often does the admin assistant check her e-mail and why?
2. How does the admin assistant categorise her e-mails?
3. Give one example of what the admin assistant uses her calendar (Outlook) for?
4. What software does the admin assistant use to keep track of statistics and run various reports?
5. State three other duties the admin assistant may carry out.
6. Why should files (both manual and computerised) be kept organised?

## ? Questions

1. Name a document that an organisation would send to an applicant to give further details of a post advertised.
2. Explain the purpose of a job description.
3. Both a job description and person specification will be produced for vacancies. Describe the information contained in each of these documents.
4. Identify two tasks/duties that will be included in the job description of an admin assistant.

5. The Human Resources department of a business issues contracts of employment. Give two pieces of information contained in the contract of employment.
6. What is identified by a skill scan?
7. Explain how a completed skill scan will be used by an organisation.

## Key questions

Download the file *Job Advert* from the Leckie & Leckie website (see page 5).

1. Complete the advert to show **two** more duties and **three** qualities/skills.
2. Print out one copy of the completed advert.
3. The application pack will contain an application form (to be completed by the applicant) and two other documents.
   **a)** Name these documents.
   **b)** List two pieces of information contained in each of these documents.
   **c)** Describe how each of these documents is used by the applicant.

## Skill

- Literacy
- Employability
- Skills for learning, life and work

## Activity

***Individually or in pairs***

Use local/national newspapers or the Internet to carry out research on three current vacancies available for admin assistants.

Using the information available, identify the:

- current salary
- location
- working hours
- tasks/duties
- qualities and skills required

***Group or whole class***

- Discuss how the information from the job adverts above differs for admin assistants working in different types of organisations.

## Summary

In this topic you have learned what tasks and duties are carried out by an admin assistant. You have also learned which skills and qualities are required to be an admin assistant.

- An admin assistant will be required to carry out a wide range of tasks and duties, for example organising events, updating and maintaining computerised records, answering the telephone and covering reception.
- An admin assistant should have good IT skills, including the use of standard office applications and emerging technologies. Skills can be identified using a skill scan and/or SWOT analysis.
- An admin assistant should possess the following qualities – have good time management, be organised and be motivated.

## Learning Checklist

| Skills, knowledge and understanding | Strength ☺ | 😐 | Weakness ☹ | Next steps |
|---|---|---|---|---|
| I understand the tasks/duties of an admin assistant. | | | | |
| I understand what a job description is and why it is used. | | | | |
| I understand the skills required of an admin assistant. | | | | |
| I understand the qualities required of an admin assistant. | | | | |
| I understand what a person specification is and why it is used. | | | | |
| I understand what a skill scan and/or SWOT analysis is and why it is used. | | | | |

# 2 Customer care

**You should already know**

- By researching the organisation of a business, I can discuss the role of departments and personnel, evaluating how they contribute to the success or failure of the business. **SOC 4-22a**

**In this chapter you will learn about:**

- The key features of good customer service.
- The benefits of good customer service.
- The impact of poor customer service.

## The key features of good customer service

### Who are an organisation's customers?

**Watch point**

Customers can be internal (other employees) or external (people who purchase goods/ services).

Customers can be both internal and external and a good admin assistant must know how to behave in relation to other employees within the organisation – internal customers – as well as people who buy the organisation's products and services – external customers.

Customer care is sometimes seen to be more important for some employees than others, but it is equally important in all areas of the organisation. For example:

- A receptionist or any employee who deals directly with external customers should have customer care as a key consideration in their job description and training.
- An admin assistant responsible for processing business documents may have little direct contact with customers, but customer satisfaction will be low if the documents contain errors.

### Customer service policy

A customer service policy is a written statement of the organisation's policy and their plans for dealing with their customers. This document is produced to ensure that customers get:

- the product/service they want
- the standard they want
- a price that is acceptable

An organisation must aim to keep customers satisfied and ensure that all customers are treated in a consistent, fair way. A customer service policy will document the organisation's policy and how they will deal with the following aspects of customer care.

- Communicating with customers:
  - Employees should respond to customer letters or e-mails promptly.
  - Employees should answer the phone politely and within an agreed number of rings.
  - Employees should keep the customer informed at all times of up-to-date information and/or any changes to the agreement.
- Ensuring the quality of customer care:
  - The organisation should provide regular customer care training for employees.
  - The organisation should provide employees with a copy of the customer care policy.
  - The organisation should regularly review the customer service policy.
- Monitoring that customer needs are satisfied:
  - The organisation should survey their customers' opinions (this could be done online, by phone or by post).
  - The organisation could use a mystery shopper to measure satisfaction.
  - The organisation could analyse loyalty card use (frequency, types of products).
- Dealing with customer complaints.
  - Employees should follow a formal procedure for dealing with all complaints.
  - Organisations should use complaints as a learning experience, in order to not to repeat the same mistakes.

Many organisations use their website to inform customers and potential customers about their customer service policy.

### Mission statement

Most organisations have a mission statement, which gives an outline of the main intentions of the organisation. It can be a

mix between a slogan and a summary of the organisation's aims. It is used to tell external customers about the organisation and its ideals. It is also used to give employees an idea or vision of what the organisation hopes to achieve and helps them to focus their work towards achieving this goal.

Most mission statements are very short – usually no longer than two or three sentences.

### Case study

Examples of mission statements from well-known organisations.

eBay: 'eBay's mission statement is to provide a global trading platform where practically anyone can trade practically anything.'

Apple: 'To produce high quality, low cost, easy to use products that incorporate high technology for the individual. We are proving that high technology does not have to be intimidating for non-computer experts.'

Arnold Clark: 'To offer genuine value for money and create high levels of customer satisfaction.'

Walt Disney: 'To make people happy.'

These are the 'one-liners', but each is supported by a set of values that set the performance standards and direct the implementation of the mission.

Walt Disney states some of their values as follows.

- Creativity, dreams and imagination.
- Fanatical attention to consistency and detail.
- Preservation and control of the Disney 'magic'.

## The features of good customer service

When we think about customers we usually mean people who buy an organisation's goods and services. However, it is just as important to ensure that an organisation's internal customers are satisfied.

Good customer service is about satisfying the needs of individuals and retaining their loyalty to the organisation.

Good customer service is essential if an organisation wants to survive in the market place, remain competitive, keep loyal customers and attract new customers.

The key features of good customer service are:

- putting the customer first
- communicating with customers effectively
- ensuring that staff are knowledgeable about products and services
- providing a good after-sales service
- dealing with complaints effectively

## The benefits of good customer service

It is important that all customers (internal and external) are treated well, as this will provide benefits for the organisation as well as the customer.

| | |
|---|---|
| **Satisfied customers** | If customers are happy with the products or services being provided they will return and recommend the organisation to others. |
| **Keeping loyal customers** | This can be done by offering customer loyalty schemes, such as the Boots Advantage Card, Nectar points, etc. |
| **Attracting new customers** | This might be as a result of a recommendation from an existing customer or persuasion through loyalty schemes or advertising. |
| **Satisfied and motivated employees** | A clear customer care strategy allows employees to deal with all customers effectively, reducing stress. |
| **Lower staff turnover** | Employees are not stressed and will stay with the organisation. |
| **Reduced costs** | The cost of recruiting new employees is not necessary. |
| **Good/improved reputation** | Recommendations from existing customers will improve the image of the organisation; if a customer has had a good experience with an organisation, they are likely to talk about it. |
| **Competitive edge** | A good reputation and/or more effective performance will mean that customers are more likely to choose that organisation rather than a competitor. |
| **Increased sales/profits** | More customers (loyal and new) will mean that the organisation will increase the value of their sales and therefore increase their profit. |

Increased sales and/or profits will result from any of the other benefits of good customer service. For example, attracting new customers will lead to an increase in sales and therefore profits. A consequence *of attracting new customers is an increase in sales/profits.*

**Watch point**

Make sure you can identify/describe **three** benefits of good customer service.

## The impact of poor customer service

Customer care is important at all levels in an organisation. A business cannot survive without customers. In the same way that good customer care benefits an organisation, poor customer care will have a negative effect.

| | |
|---|---|
| **Dissatisfied customers** | If customers are unhappy about the products or services being provided, they will not return and will tell others of their dissatisfaction. |
| **Loss of customers** | Dissatisfied customers will look for products or services elsewhere. |
| **Bad publicity** | Dissatisfied customers will talk, and leave bad reviews! |
| **Demotivated employees** | Employees who do not receive appropriate customer-care training, or have not been advised of the organisation's customer-care strategy, may make mistakes, not deal with customers effectively, and this will lead to stress. |
| **High staff turnover** | Unhappy employees will leave to work elsewhere. |
| **Increased costs** | The costs of recruiting/training new staff will be high. |
| **Poor reputation** | The organisation will gain a poor reputation through bad publicity and customers/employees talking of their dissatisfaction/ demotivation. |
| **Poor competitive edge** | Customers will be more likely to choose a competitor as they are performing more effectively. |
| **Decreased sales/profits** | Fewer customers (the loss of loyal customers and not attracting new customers) will result in lower sales and therefore lower profits. |
| **Legal action** | Employees not complying with consumer legislation may lead to customers taking legal action. |

**Watch point**

A **consequence** is what happens **because** of poor customer service.

**Watch point**

Make sure you can identify/ describe **three** consequences of poor customer service.

Any one of the above could lead to the organisation ceasing to exist.

Decreased sales/profits will result from any of the other effects of poor customer service. For example, losing loyal customers will lead to a decrease in sales and therefore profits. A consequence of losing loyal customers is a decrease in sales/ profits.

## Case study

Read the case study below.

***Why is customer service so important to Portakabin?***

Customers of a business can be new ones or current ones returning to buy more. The significance of good customer service can be shown in financial terms, as it costs at least five times as much to win a new customer as it does to keep a current one. Much of the profits of most businesses rely on repeat custom.

### Make the Link

In the Organising and supporting events chapter you will be required to consider customers' opinions following an event.

It costs as much to gain ONE new client as to keep FIVE existing ones

Portakabin may be the market leader, but if it had poor customer service, clients could switch to one of its rivals. The bulk of the company's profits come from repeat sales, so it is vital to keep clients content. This helps the business to compete. Due to the commitment Portakabin has shown in providing a first-class level of service, its service levels have become, in its own words, 'legendary'.

**Legendary customer service**

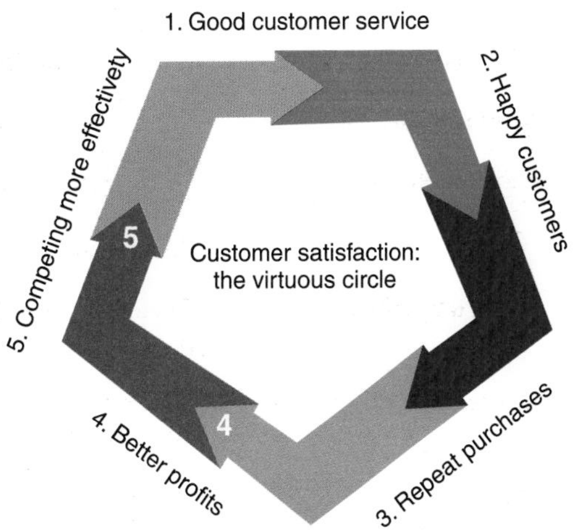


Customers can be either internal or external. Internal customers are people within the business who depend on other parts of it. For example, continued good sales (in the sales department) may depend on the quality of the product (in the production department). External customers are those who come to buy products. Portakabin knows that if its internal customers deliver excellent service, external customer service excellence will follow – each member of the business is able to contribute to better service. To this end, each department has been encouraged to create its own internal customer charter, and a first-class service is the target of all internal departments.

Answer the following questions:

1. Identify an example of internal customers in the Portakabin organisation.
2. Why is it important to keep loyal customers?
3. What would happen if Portakabin had poor customer service?
4. Where does the organisation believe most of its profits come from?
5. Give **two** more benefits to the organisation of good customer service.

## Questions

1. State the purpose of a mission statement.
2. Suggest why a mission statement is important to an organisation.
3. Explain why customer loyalty is important to an organisation.
4. Describe **two** benefits of good customer service to an organisation.
5. Describe the impact on an organisation of poor customer service.

## Skill

- Literacy
- Employability
- Skills for learning, life and work

## Key questions

1. Give an example of an internal customer.
2. Give an example of an external customer.
3. Describe a customer service policy.
4. Give **two** examples of how an organisation might monitor customer satisfaction.
5. Explain how a mission statement is useful to the employees of an organisation.
6. Identify **three** key features of good customer service.
7. Good customer service is important to an organisation. Explain the implications for an organisation of poor customer service.
8. Suggest **three** effects of poor customer service to an organisation.

## Activity

***Individually, do one of the following activities***

1. Produce a poster to promote good customer service using WP/DTP software. Include:
   **(a)** two benefits of good customer service
   **(b)** two tips to ensure good customer service
2. Download the file *Hotel Survey Form* from the Leckie & Leckie website (see page 5).
   **(a)** Complete the form by carrying out the instructions provided in the comments.
   **(b)** Delete the comments.
   **(c)** Save and print one copy of the form.

***In pairs***

Discuss the advantages/disadvantages of different methods of monitoring customer satisfaction and complete the following table.

| | Postal survey | Telephone survey | Online survey | Mystery shopper |
|---|---|---|---|---|
| **Speed** | Slow | | | |
| **Cost** | Expensive | | | |
| **Level of response** | Low | | | |
| **Depth of response** | Low | | | |
| **Advantages** | Provides a written record | | | |
| **Disadvantages** | Low return rate<br>Expensive | | | |

***Group or whole class***

Discuss why customer service is so important to any organisation. Discuss the consequences of good and poor customer service.

## Summary

In this topic you have learned what customer care is.

- Organisations have internal customers (for example, employees in other departments) and external customers (for example, people who purchase goods/services).
- A mission statement is a summary of an organisation's aims and is used to let customers and employees know their intentions.
- Organisations must have a customer service policy to ensure that all customers are aware of the organisation's policy and their plans for dealing with customers. This includes communication with customers, monitoring customer satisfaction, dealing with complaints.
- The key features of good customer service are about putting the customer first, providing customer satisfaction, communicating with customers effectively, ensuring that staff are knowledgeable about products and services, providing a good after-sales service and dealing with customer complaints effectively.
- Good customer service will result in keeping loyal customers, attracting new customers, good reputation, competitive edge, increased sales/profits.
- Poor customer service will result in losing customers, not attracting newcustomers, poor reputation, losing competitive edge and decreased sales/profits.

## Learning Checklist

| Skills, knowledge and understanding | Strength ☺ | 😐 | Weakness ☹ | Next steps |
|---|---|---|---|---|
| I understand what an internal customer is. | | | | |
| I understand what an external customer is. | | | | |
| I understand what a customer service strategy is. | | | | |
| I understand what a mission statement is. | | | | |
| I understand why a mission statement is used. | | | | |
| I understand the key features of good customer service. | | | | |
| I understand the effects of good customer service. | | | | |
| I understand the impact of poor customer service. | | | | |

# 3 Health and safety

**You should already know**

- Whilst working in a simulated or real workplace, I can examine my work environment, considering office layout, ergonomics factors, and health and safety legislation. **TCH 4-07b**
- Steps that an individual will take to ensure their own health and safety.
- Fire evacuation procedures carried out in your centre/school.

**In this chapter you will learn about:**

- Hazards in the workplace and measures taken to ensure safe practice.
- The procedure to be followed when an accident occurs (and how to complete the required documentation).
- What is meant by an organisational health and safety policy and what it includes.
- The use of induction training to cover health and safety issues.
- Current UK health and safety legislation and what employers and employees should do in relation to these acts.

## Identification of hazards and measures to ensure safe practice

Accidents can occur within the workplace. It is important that all hazards are minimised in order to reduce the number of accidents that occur.

Major injuries can be caused by:

- slips or trips (from trailing cables, open filing cabinets, etc.)
- falling (when trying to reach the top of a cupboard or shelf)
- poor lifting and handling techniques.

Common sense should prevail at all times. The following checklist could be used to remind employees of the common sense approach they should take towards health and safety. Notices should also be placed in appropriate areas to remind staff of their health and safety duties.

*Safety checklist*

| | |
|---|---|
| **To prevent slips or trips, employees should:**<br>• position desks to avoid trailing cables or use a cable management system<br>• position filing cabinets away from the door<br>• never store heavy materials in a hard-to-reach place (provide a step ladder if required)<br>• mop up any liquids that have been spilled (use a danger sign if the floor is still wet)<br>• keep passageways free from obstacles | ✓ |
| **To prevent fires, employees should:**<br>• keep liquids away from computer equipment<br>• never overload power sockets (reposition furniture or install more power points if required)<br>• report any faults immediately<br>• empty waste bins regularly<br>• smoke only in designated areas<br>• never prop open fire doors | ✓ |
| **General warnings:**<br>• Never attempt to fix equipment unless fully trained to do so.<br>• Report loose flooring.<br>• Employees should always keep their own work areas tidy. | ✓ |

If an accident does occur within the organisation, an **accident report form** and an **accident book** must be completed. The accident report form may be completed either by a witness to the accident or the person involved in the accident. Examples of an accident report form and an accident book are over the page.

**Watch point**

Practise completing the following forms because you may be asked to complete one of them in the assignment.

| Accident report form | |
|---|---|
| Name of injured person | Amy Taylor |
| Date of birth | 16/9/88 |
| Position in the organisation | Finance Manager |
| Date and time of incident | 22 June 2013, 11 am |
| Brief description of accident (continue on separate sheet if required) | Tripped over trailing cables |
| Place of accident | Reception |
| Details of injury | Broken wrist, sprained ankle |
| First aid treatment (if given) | Ice pack on wrist and ankle |
| Was the injured person taken to hospital/doctor | Taken to Glasgow General Hospital – Accident and Emergency department |
| Name(s) and position(s) of person(s) present when accident occurred | Chloe Pearce, Human Resources Manager |
| Signature of person reporting the accident .................................................... | |
| Date .................................................... | |

**Accident book**

| Date | Time | Location | Name of injured person | Witness | Details of accident and action taken |
|---|---|---|---|---|---|
| 12/4/13 | 3.30 pm | Sales department | Kirstin Dolan | Lewis Smith | Fell whilst trying to reach material on high shelf. Head bandaged and taken to hospital. |
| 22/6/13 | 11 am | Reception | Amy Taylor | Chloe Pearce | Tripped over trailing cables. Ice pack placed on wrist and ankle. Taken to hospital. |

The accident report form and accident book may be stored on the organisation's internal computer network (intranet), which would allow employees to access it, complete it on the computer and e-mail it immediately to the relevant person.

It is very important that the organisation maintains a record of all accidents – if there are too many accidents occurring then the Health and Safety Executive will investigate health and safety practices within the firm.

## The Health and Safety Executive (HSE)

The Health and Safety Executive work with local authorities to check the standards of health, safety and welfare in organisations as well as giving advice on how to prevent people becoming ill because of, or being injured at, work.

HSE inspectors can carry out random spot checks on organisations. The following sanctions and penalties can be imposed where health and safety legislation has been breached.

- An improvement notice may be served – this states what the organisation should do to comply with health and safety law, why, and a deadline will be given for compliance.
- A prohibition notice may be served – where premises that are considered to be a serious risk to personal safety may be closed.
- Prosecution – failure to comply with an improvement notice or prohibition order can result in either a fine of £20,000 or up to 6 months imprisonment.

**Watch point**

The HSE enforces all current health and safety legislation.

## Health and safety policy statement

An organisation that employs five or more people must, by law, have a written health and safety policy. Describing how the organisation will manage health and safety lets staff and others know that the organisation is committed to keeping all staff healthy and safe. The policy should include the following information:

- The name of the person(s) responsible for carrying out health and safety checks within the organisation – and how often this will occur.
- Appropriate health and safety training to be given to employees.
- The organisation's evacuation procedure.
- How often employees will be consulted on day-to-day health and safety conditions.
- Details of the maintenance of equipment.

**Watch point**

A policy statement is a document that explains procedures carried out by an organisation, i.e. how things are done.

The Health and Safety at Work Act 1974 states that all employees must have access to the organisation's health and safety policy. The policy may be stored on the organisation's intranet to ensure ease of access by all employees, this also make the regular

**Watch point**

Induction training is training given to **new** employees to introduce them to the organisation.

updating of the policy easier, as organisations must review and revise their policy as often as necessary.

Organisations may provide employees with a copy of their health and safety policy during their **induction training**. Health and safety procedures will be explained in detail during induction training, and, evacuation and first-aid procedures will also be explained.

## Current legislation

### Health and Safety at Work Act 1974

| Responsibilities of an employee | Responsibilities of an organisation |
|---|---|
| • Take reasonable care of their own health and safety and the health and safety of others.<br>• Co-operate with the employer on health and safety matters.<br>• Do not misuse or interfere with anything provided for employees' health and safety. | • Ensure safe methods of working.<br>• Ensure safe working conditions.<br>• Ensure all employees receive information and training on health and safety.<br>• Ensure that equipment is safe and properly stored.<br>• Provide protective clothing where necessary. |

**Watch point**

The Health and Safety (Display Screen Equipment) Regulations only apply to employees who use VDUs for a significant part of their working day.

### Health and Safety (Display Screen Equipment) Regulations 1992

This act is designed to minimise the potential risks associated with the use of visual display units (VDUs), including:

Eye Strain

Headaches

Repetitive strain injury

Backache

| Responsibilities of an employee | Responsibilities of an organisation |
|---|---|
| Avoid potential health hazards by:<br>• Making use of adjustment facilities for the VDU.<br>• Adjusting chair for maximum comfort.<br>• Arranging desk and screen to avoid glare. | • Assess workstation requirements.<br>• Provide adjustable seating.<br>• Provide adjustable and tilting screens.<br>• Provide health and safety training for employees.<br>• Organise daily work of VDU users so that there are regular rest breaks or changes in activity. |

## Health and Safety (First Aid) Regulations 1981

Organisations are required to:

- provide a well-stocked first aid box
- appoint a first aider (it is recommended that there should be one for every 50–100 employees)
- inform staff of first aid procedures
- keep a record of all accidents/incidents

## Fire Precautions (Places of Work) Regulations 1995

Organisations are required to:

- assess fire risks in the organisation
- provide appropriate fire-fighting equipment such as fire extinguishers
- check and maintain fire-fighting equipment
- provide warning systems (and check them regularly)
- train employees in fire procedures
- regularly check evacuation procedures (regular fire drills would help check that routes are appropriate, timings are acceptable, etc.)

### Watch point

Fire evacuation notices should be displayed prominently for all employees and visitors to see – they should be displayed in all areas, including the reception area.

### Make the link

- In Technical Education we learn how to remain safe in a busy, working environment.
- In Modern Studies we learn how laws protect citizens.
- In English we learn the importance of using appropriate language depending on what we are doing.

## Activity

Most organisations are committed to ensure the health, safety and well-being of all their employees, customers and others who visit or work on their premises. Do **one** of the following activities:

1. Use the Internet to research a well-known organisation's health and safety policy. Use the information available to prepare a brief summary of your chosen organisation's health and safety policy.
2. Watch the following video clip and answer the questions that follow. http://www.youtube.com/watch?v=23IlZMEZnNk
   - **(a)** What hazards can often be found in an office?
   - **(b)** Identify obstacles that may cause tripping hazards.
   - **(c)** State **two** causes of slipping accidents in the office.
   - **(d)** Identify **three** ways of eliminating hazards in the office.
   - **(e)** What should be done with electrical cords/wires/cables to prevent slips?
   - **(f)** What should be used to reach high places in the office?

## ? Questions

1. State two ways to prevent slips or trips in the workplace.
2. Identify the documents that should be completed if an accident does occur within the workplace?
3. State why these documents should be stored on an organisation's intranet?
4. Explain the purpose of the Health and Safety Executive (HSE).
5. List what information should be contained in an organisation's health and safety policy.
6. State what is meant by the term **induction training**.
7. Complete the following table with the responsibilities of an employer and an employee with regard to the Health and Safety at Work Act 1974. The first one has been completed for you.

| Responsibilities of an employee | Responsibilities of an organisation |
|---|---|
| Take reasonable care of their own health and safety and the health and safety of others. | Ensure safe methods of working. |
| | |
| | |

8. Identify **two** responsibilities of an employee and an organisation stated in the Health and Safety (Display Screen Equipment) Regulations 1992.
9. Outline the responsibilities of an organisation that are required by the Health and Safety (First Aid) Regulations 1981.
10. Suggest **two** steps that should be taken to prevent injury from fire within an organisation.

## Key questions

1. Outline **two** ways the following pieces of legislation are being breached in the picture above.
   (a) Health and Safety at Work Act 1974
   (b) Health and Safety (Display Screen Equipment) Regulations 1992
2. Describe **two** responsibilities of an employee under the Health and Safety at Work Act 1974.
3. Organisations must comply with the Health and Safety at Work Act 1974 and the Health and Safety (Display Screen Equipment) Regulations 1992.
   (a) Name **two** other pieces of health and safety legislation an organisation should comply with.
   (b) For each of the acts you have mentioned in (a) describe the responsibilities of the organisation.

### Skill

- Literacy
- Communication
- Information Technology
- Presentation
- Employability
- Skills for learning, life and work

## Activity

***Individually or in pairs***

Prepare a checklist to be used to identify any hazards in your school/centre using WP/DTP software.

Use the following layout for your checklist. An example for each subheading has been completed for you.

| Name of School/Centre ............................................................................ | | |
|---|---|---|
| Date of Inspection .................................................................................. | | |
| Name and position of Inspector(s)............................................................. | | |
| | Yes | No |
| **Fire safety** | | |
| **1.** Is appropriate fire-fighting equipment available? | | |
| **2.** | | |
| **3.** | | |
| **4.** | | |
| **First aid** | | |
| **1.** Is a fully-stocked first aid box available? | | |
| **2.** | | |
| **3.** | | |
| **4.** | | |
| **General hazard** | | |
| **1.** Is a cable management system in operation? | | |
| **2.** | | |
| **3.** | | |
| **4.** | | |

***Group or whole class***

Using the findings from the activity above, prepare a report summarising any health and safety concerns you have. E-mail your report to the appropriate health and safety representative in your school/centre.

## Summary

In this chapter you have learned about hazards within the workplace and how to minimise these hazards.

- If an accident does occur an accident report form and an accident book report should be completed.
- The HSE work with your local authority to ensure that all health and safety laws are followed; if they are not, they have sanctions which they can apply to an organisation.
- An organisation will have a health and safety policy statement that shows their commitment to health and safety within the organisation.
- Employees must have access to the health and safety policy – it is often given to new employees when they undertake induction training.
- You should also know the various pieces of legislation that cover health and safety in the workplace. In particular, the relevant responsibilities of employees and employers.

## Learning Checklist

| Skills, knowledge and understanding | Strength ☺ | 😐 | Weakness ☹ | Next steps |
|---|---|---|---|---|
| I understand the hazards in the workplace and measures taken to ensure safe practice. | | | | |
| I understand the procedure to be followed when an accident occurs and how to complete the required documentation. | | | | |
| I understand what is meant by an organisational health and safety policy and what it includes. | | | | |
| I understand the use of induction training to cover health and safety issues. | | | | |
| I understand current UK health and safety legislation and what employers and employees should do in relation to these acts. | | | | |

# 4 Security of people, property and information

**You should already know**

- From your own experience and knowledge, measures used to protect people. For example, staff wearing ID badges, buzzers to enter school, etc.
- From your own experience and knowledge, measures used to protect property, for example burglar alarms.

**In this chapter you will learn about:**

- Organisational procedures used to protect people.
- Organisational procedures used to protect property.
- Organisational procedures used to protect both paper-based and electronic information.
- The Data Protection Act 1998 and The Computer Misuse Act 1990.

## Security of people

As the reception area is usually located at the entrance of an organisation, it plays a crucial role in the security of an organisation.

The following security measures are taken by the receptionist.

| | |
|---|---|
| **Checking staff ID badges or security passes** | All staff should be issued with an ID badge (which contains information such as their name, photograph, job title, department) when they start working in the organisation. This should be shown to the receptionist each time they wish to gain entry to the building. Staff should also keep their ID badges prominently displayed throughout the day. |
| **Monitoring CCTV** | Areas within and outwith the building can be observed and recorded. |
| **Controlling the entry system** | Anyone wishing to enter the building must first contact the receptionist who will check their identity before the door is opened. |
| **Appointments book**<br>**Visitors' book**<br>**Staff in/out book** | These records provide information on who has been in the organisation at specific times. |
| **Issuing visitors' badges** | These allow authorised visitors to be identified by staff. Visitors should not be left unsupervised when in the organisation. |

While the above examples demonstrate how the reception area contributes to the security of the organisation (and the people in these areas), the following security measures may also be used within the organisation:

| | |
|---|---|
| **Keypads**<br>**Combination locks**<br>**Swipe cards** | Access is restricted to those who are authorised and who have the appropriate number/card. Swipe cards can be programmed to allow an employee access to certain areas that they have permission to be in and bar access to others. Similarly, staff may hold the keypad/combination number for only the areas for which they require access, and not for others. |
| **Locked doors** | Only authorised members of staff will be given a key. There must be a record kept of all key holders. |
| **Staff uniform** | This makes unauthorised visitors easily identifiable. |

**Watch point**

At National 4 you should know the responsibilities of the employee –wearing ID badges, signing the staff in/out book.

At National 5 you should know the responsibilities of the organisation –issue staff with ID badges, provide a staff in/out book.

## Security of property

In addition to the measures mentioned on previous pages (the security of people), the following measures could also be taken to ensure the security of property.

| | |
|---|---|
| **Attach equipment to desk** | Computer keyboards/monitors etc. could be bolted to desks. |
| **Mark equipment with UV (ultra violet) pens** | In event of property being stolen, police would be able to quickly find out the owner. This may be used as a deterrent to thieves. |
| **Keep an inventory of equipment** | Keeping a record of equipment means that if any equipment goes missing it will quickly be noticed. This may act as a deterrent to thieves. |
| **Security cables** | These can be used with portable laptops/notebooks/netbooks. A steel cable secures the item to any solid or fixed object. |
| **Ensure that office doors and windows are locked** | This must be done before leaving the premises, particularly by the last member of staff in the building. |
| **Alarm** | This may be set at night when the building is empty. The police may be contacted directly if the alarm is activated. |
| **Security guard** | A security guard may patrol the premises (usually at night) to protect the building. Security lighting could also be used at night to detect motion. |
| **Security blinds** | Strong shutters can be placed over doors and windows to prevent burglary, theft and vandalism. |

## Security of information

### Securing information stored manually

**Watch point**
Information may be paper-based (manual) or electronic (on computer).

Access to areas of the building where confidential information is kept should be restricted. This can be through the use of locked doors, or key pads, combination locks, swipe cards, etc. Visitors should never be left unsupervised at any time.

Filing cabinets that hold confidential information should be locked and only authorised personnel should have access to the keys. Confidential information should never be left lying around (for example at the photocopier or printer) and it should either be filed securely or shredded immediately after use.

### Security of information stored electronically

**Watch point**
Passwords should never be shared and must be changed regularly.

Each individual computer user should be issued with a unique username and a password – this makes it easier to monitor use of the computer system. Usernames and passwords will control access to:

- **Computers** – the computer can only be used when the username/password is entered correctly.

- **Files** – each username and password will give the user access to the information they require (this is often used in schools for example, the ICT co-ordinator will have access to much more information than a pupil). This is often referred to as access rights or access level passwords.

Passwords can also be used with a screensaver. Confidential information should never be left on the screen for others to see – either a password-protected screensaver should be activated or shut-down procedures should be followed.

Other methods of protecting information held on computer include:

- saving files as read-only documents so they cannot be changed by other users
- ensuring storage media (flash drives/pens, CDs, etc.) should be labelled and stored in a locked drawer
- inserting security ID cards/keys into the computer (these are only held by authorised users)
- using measures such as voiceprint/fingerprint recognition or iris/signature scanners
- installing anti-virus software to ensure that no computer virus can corrupt the data
- using encryption software to code the data – if the computer is hacked then the data is meaningless to the hacker

**Watch point**

All data held on computer should be backed-up on a regular basis. This means taking a second copy of the data that is then stored separately.

## Data Protection Act 1998

The Data Protection Act applies to information stored both manually and electronically. It protects both the **data subject** (the person about whom the information is stored) and the **data user** (the person or organisation that stores the information). Data users must be registered with the Data Protection Registrar and follow the principles of the Act.

The Act states that personal data must be:

- fairly and lawfully processed
- used for the registered purpose only
- adequate, relevant and not excessive
- accurate
- kept for no longer than is necessary
- kept securely

- processed in line with the individual's legal rights
- transferred to countries outside the European Economic Area only if the individual's rights can be assured.

Data must be made available to the data subject upon request.

If an organisation fails to comply with the Data Protection Act, it may be prosecuted and fined.

### Computer Misuse Act 1990

The purpose of the Computer Misuse Act 1990 is to prohibit unlawful access to computer systems. This act makes it illegal to:

- access computers without permission (e.g. hacking)
- access computers with the intention of committing a criminal offence
- access computers to change or alter details without permission.

#### Make the link

- In Computing we learn about laws/legislation affecting the storage of information.
- In Modern Studies we learn about the importance of being protected by laws.

### Organisations' own security measures

The size and nature of business conducted by an organisation will determine the security measures it will take. An organisation will make use of a wide range of security measures (such as those described in this chapter) in order to protect the **people** who work and visit the organisation, its **property** and the **information** stored in the organisation.

#### Activity

Use the BBC Bitesize website (follow the links to ICT) to revise, attempt the activity, and then test your knowledge of data security.

1. Explain why the reception area plays a crucial role in the security of an organisation.
2. Describe three security measures taken by the receptionist.
3. State how keypads/combination locks/swipecards can restrict unauthorised access.
4. Describe three security measures taken by an organisation to protect property.
5. List two ways that usernames and passwords can restrict access to information.
6. List three other methods of protecting information held on computer.
7. State what is meant by the term 'back-up'.
8. Outline the main principles of the Data Protection Act 1998.
9. Give the purpose of the Computer Misuse Act 1990.

## Key questions

Download the file *Staff Handbook* from the Leckie & Leckie website (see page 5).

1. Update the extract from the staff handbook with relevant information on employee and organisational responsibilities with regard to security within the organisation.
2. Print one copy of the updated staff handbook.

## Skill

- Decision-making
- ICT
- Literacy
- Employability
- Skills for learning, life and work

## Activity

***Individually or in pairs***

Get ready to be quizzed! But first you need to be the quizmaster!

Either individually or with your partner, prepare a quiz on the security of people, property and information. You could search the Internet for ideas on different formats – perhaps even prepare the quiz on the computer – but whatever you do, ensure that you have all your answers ready.

Give another person or pair the quiz and see how they perform – while you try theirs.

***Group or whole class***

Work in groups to prepare questions (and solutions) that could be used as a whole-class quiz. Your teacher will select an equal number of questions from each group and you can have a battle to see which group are the experts in security of people, property and information. (You never know – your teacher may even provide a prize!)

## Summary

Organisations view the security of people, property and information very seriously. They employ a range of measures to ensure that they are kept secure. Organisations should also ensure they comply with the Data Protection Act 1998 and The Computer Misuse Act 1990.

***To ensure people are kept secure***

Reception staff may:

- check staff ID badges
- monitor CCTV
- use intercoms, entryphones or buzzer systems

(continued)

- keep an appointments book, visitors' book, or staff in and out book
- issue visitors' badges

**Other measures include the use of keypads, combination locks, swipe cards, locked doors and staff uniforms.**

*To ensure property is kept secure*
The following measures may be taken:

- attaching equipment to desks
- marking equipment with UV pens
- keeping an inventory of equipment
- using security cables
- ensuring all office doors and windows are locked
- using an alarm
- employing a security guard
- having security blinds

*To ensure paper-based information is kept secure*
An organisation will:

- restrict access to areas of the building where confidential information is kept
- lock filing cabinets
- remind staff never to leave confidential information lying around
- file/shred confidential information after use

*To ensure computer-based information is kept secure*
An organisation will:

- issue unique usernames and passwords to individuals
- encrypt confidential information
- save files as read-only files
- use security ID cards, keys, voiceprint/fingerprint recognition, iris/signature scanners
- install anti-virus software
- ensure storage media is locked away

## Learning Checklist

| Skills, knowledge and understanding | Strength ☺ | 😐 | Weakness ☹ | Next steps |
|---|---|---|---|---|
| I understand organisational procedures used to protect people. | | | | |
| I understand organisational procedures used to protect property. | | | | |
| I understand organisational procedures used to protect both paper-based and electronic information. | | | | |
| I understand The Data Protection Act 1998 and The Computer Misuse Act 1990. | | | | |

# 5 Organising and supporting events

**You should already know**

- How to use word processing software to prepare documents.
- How to use spreadsheet software.
- How to use database software – update, search and create mailmerge.
- How to use presentation software.

**In this chapter you will learn about:**

- What an event is.
- Tasks undertaken by an admin assistant when planning for the event.
- Tasks undertaken by an admin assistant during the event.
- Tasks undertaken by an admin assistant following the event.

## Carrying out planning tasks

### What is an event?

An event is an important, planned occasion. Examples of events include:

- meetings
- interviews
- award ceremonies
- fundraising event
- sales event
- press conference
- training sessions

An admin assistant will be expected to support events planned by an organisation, this includes completing a range of tasks and producing various documents relating to an event.

An admin assistant will usually break down the administration of an event into three areas:

1. **Planning tasks** – tasks that carried out **before** the event takes place.

2. **Supporting the event** – tasks that relate to the **day of the event**.
3. **Follow-up tasks** – tasks that are completed **after** the event has taken place.

## Planning the event

To ensure a successful event, planning is key!

An Event Brief is usually received by the admin assistant to explain the purpose of the event/meeting, for example whether it is a sales conference, training session and so on. The brief should also outline some basic information for the event, such as the budget, who should be asked to attend, dates that could be considered, possible venue locations, etc.

Once this has been received, the admin assistant can start to plan for the event.

A **to-do list** or a **priorities list** will make it easier for the admin assistant to focus on what needs to be done and when. The admin assistant will create a list of tasks to be undertaken for the event and will then sort these tasks into order of urgency (priority). They should refer to the priorities list on a regular basis to ensure nothing is missed out.

One of the first items on the priorities list will be to select a suitable date. Consideration must be given to things that may affect the number of people going to the event, such as public holidays or competing events. Once a date has been selected it should be entered into the (electronic) diaries of affected members of staff immediately (to avoid double bookings).

The venue should then be chosen. The following should be considered when selecting a venue:

- Is the date selected available?
- The number of people attending.
- Ease of access for all attendees. (Is it near a bus/train station? Is parking available?)
- Room layout.
- What IT and audio/visual facilities are available (laptops, data projectors, flip charts etc.)
- Is catering available? Will any special dietary requirements be catered for?
- Budget – is the cost of the venue within the specified budget?
- Does the venue comply with health and safety legislation, for example are there toilet facilities available?

**Watch point**

The Internet is a good source of information on venues. As well as checking availability instantly, many websites will also provide information on catering, room layouts, IT facilities and will show photographs of rooms available for events.

**Watch point**

Information about catering should be gathered from attendees beforehand to ensure that all special dietary requirements are catered for (vegetarian, vegan, gluten-free, etc.)

**Watch point**

The admin assistant may also be required to gather travel information for attendees, such as train/bus times, and venue maps.

A number of venues can be researched before finding the most suitable one; and once a venue has been selected it should be **booked**. This can be done using e-mail, fax, telephone or letter. The admin assistant should ensure that written **confirmation of the booking** is received, whether via e-mail, post or fax.

Keeping within budget is very important. Some costs include: hiring the venue, hiring speakers, catering, stationery, marketing, transport, staff costs, equipment hire. Spreadsheet software should be used to keep a track of the costs of the event.

Invitations should be sent out to potential attendees, for example key/guest speakers. If the event is a regular occurrence, such as an annual general meeting (AGM), a **Notice of Meeting** and an **Agenda** should be prepared and sent to those who are eligible to attend. An Agenda is a document that lists the topics to be discussed at the meeting in the order in which the discussions should take place.

**Notice of Meeting**

A meeting of the Perth Curling Club will be held in the Conference Suite, Perth Grand Hotel on 21 May 2013 at 7.30 pm.

**Agenda**

1. Apologies for absence.
2. Minutes of previous meeting.
3. Matters arising.
4. Fundraising for new equipment.
5. Scottish Curling Championship.
6. Any other business.
7. Date of next meeting.

Michelle Darroch
Secretary
28 April 2013

**Watch point**

When preparing advertising material, ensure all important information such as the date, time, cost etc. is included and highlighted.

If the event is open to the public or is not a regular occurrence then promotional/advertising material must be prepared – this may include adverts to be placed in local/national newspapers or flyers to be placed in appropriate places that potential delegates may see.

Once who will be attending the event has been established, a database with details of the attendees should be created. This will help in the production of name badges and place cards, as the mail merge facility can be used. It will also be used on the day of the event to record the actual attendance.

The admin assistant now has the required information to create a room plan – the venue and the attendees. It is now possible to create the room plan, considering where IT and audio/visual facilities are available, where the guest speaker(s) should be seated and where attendees should sit.

The admin assistant may also be responsible for preparing a presentation for the guest speaker using presentation software. This should be e-mailed to the guest speaker well in advance of the event to give them time to rehearse their speech.

If attendees are to receive information at the event, the admin assistant should ensure that an attendee pack is prepared.

To-do list/Priorities list of tasks to be completed before the event
Completed
1. Check event brief for basic information. √
2. Select suitable date and enter into (electronic) diaries. √
3. Create a spreadsheet for event costs. √
4. Research suitable venues. √
5. Select and book venue. √
6. Send invitation to guest speaker(s). √
7. Send out Notice of Meeting and Agenda or promotional materials for event. √
8. Prepare presentation for guest speaker. √
9. Create an attendee database. √
10. Create name badges/place cards etc. √
11. Create a room plan. √
12. Attendee packs prepared. √

## Supporting the event – tasks that relate to the day of the event

The admin assistant should arrive at the venue early to ensure that everything required for the event to run smoothly is ready by the time attendees arrive.

The admin assistant should bring all relevant documentation to the event, such as:

- name badges
- place cards
- the room plan
- attendee packs
- the attendee database
- the presentation for the guest speaker

Before the event takes place, all direction signs should be placed in relevant areas, the room should be set out according to the plan already created, placecards should be set out and the IT facilities checked.

An attendance desk should be set up so that attendees can report to **register** and receive their name badges and attendee packs. The attendee database could be used at this stage to record attendance. The admin assistant should also check with the management team of the centre that catering requirements have been arranged.

During the event, the admin assistant should assist guest speakers and attendees with any questions/queries.

If the event is a meeting the admin assistant will be required to take **Minutes of the Meeting** – a formal record of discussions that take place.

## Follow-up tasks

Once the event has taken place the admin assistant should ensure that the venue has been tidied and any equipment that was borrowed has been returned.

It is important to evaluate the success of the event. **Evaluation Forms** should be prepared and sent to attendees to gather their feedback on the event. Attendees are often asked to complete the evaluation form at the end of the event or they can be e-mailed it for completion at a later date.

| Evaluation form - Training event<br>Date of event:<br>Venue: | | | | | |
|---|---|---|---|---|---|
| How satisfied were you with the following?<br>(Please circle as appropriate.) | Very satisfied | | | Dissatisfied | |
| | ☺ | | 😐 | | ☹ |
| The information distributed before the event. | 5 | 4 | 3 | 2 | 1 |
| The organisation of the day. | 5 | 4 | 3 | 2 | 1 |
| The venue and facilities. | 5 | 4 | 3 | 2 | 1 |
| The arrangements and quality of the catering. | 5 | 4 | 3 | 2 | 1 |
| The presentations that were delivered at the venue. | 5 | 4 | 3 | 2 | 1 |
| The time-keeping at the event. | 5 | 4 | 3 | 2 | 1 |
| The helpfulness of staff at this event. | 5 | 4 | 3 | 2 | 1 |
| Please indicate what you think could have improved this event. | | | | | |

Once the Evaluation Forms have been received it is important that they are reviewed. The admin assistant can then take the feedback into consideration when planning the next event – to ensure that the next event is even more successful!

Management are often interested in how the event was perceived and may ask the admin assistant to prepare a brief **report** on the event and the feedback given by attendees. This can include charts, etc.

If the event was a meeting the admin assistant should prepare the Minutes of Meeting using word processing software as soon as is possible (to ensure they do not forget any discussion at the meeting). These minutes should then be sent to the Chairperson (the person in charge of the meeting). Often **Action Minutes** are also prepared, these are not as formal as Minutes of Meetings but record tasks to be carried out, who is responsible for carrying out the tasks and the dates by which they should be completed.

**Thank you letters** should be sent to the venue and to guest speakers. Guest speakers will appreciate the courtesy and may return in future to speak at another one of the organisation's events.

The attendee database should be checked to ensure it has been updated with the actual people who were present at the event.

The spreadsheet should be updated with **actual costs** of the event. A comparison of actual cost with **budgeted costs** (expected) is useful in order to find out if there were any areas of over- or under-spending. This will help with future event planning.

An organisation will want to share news of its successful event by placing information about it on their website, on social media, or perhaps in a newsletter – this may encourage future participants.

## Make the link

- In the Administrative Practices unit you will draw on the knowledge and understanding of all the earlier outcomes to plan/organise successful events.
- In the IT Solutions for Administrators unit you will develop skills on a variety of software packages which will be used when organising events.
- In the Communication in Administration unit you will develop skills in researching information on the Internet and different methods of communicating.
- You may be involved with a (school) club that organises events to raise funds.

## Activity

The school charities committee is holding a cake and candy stall to raise funds for local charities. As a member of this committee you have agreed to carry out the following tasks in preparation for this event:

- Access the electronic diary and choose a suitable date/time for this event. The committee would like the event to take place on the first Friday of next month during the school lunch break. Enter the appropriate details in the electronic diary and print a copy of this in weekly view.
- Prepare a poster to advertise this event throughout the school. Print a copy.
- Prepare an e-mail to be sent to each member of the committee, confirming the date and providing them with a copy of the poster for their feedback. Print a copy of this e-mail.
- Prepare name badges for each member of the committee – one for yourself and five others (use your classmates' names).

## ? Questions

1. Identify the software that should be used to carry out research for a suitable venue for an event.
2. Explain what an admin assistant should do to identify a suitable date for a departmental meeting.
3. Posters are a good way of drawing attention to an upcoming event. Word processing or DTP software can be used to produce posters. Identify **three** features of these packages that are used to enhance such posters.

**4.** A Notice of Meeting and Agenda must be issued to all attendees. Describe **two** different ways these can be prepared/issued efficiently.

**5.** It is important when organising an event that all costs are within budget. State how this can be done.

**6.** Identify ways that an attendee can make sure that they do not forget about an upcoming event.

**7.** Documents sent to other organisations must create a good impression. Suggest **two** ways to ensure this is done.

**8.** Give two examples of documents that may be prepared by an admin assistant following an event.

## ★ Key questions

You are employed by Caledonian Ltd in Dumbarton. Your line manager has asked you to organise a training day for all administrative staff.

Download the folder *Key Question Files* from the Leckie & Leckie website (see page 5) and complete the following tasks.

**1.** Planning/preparing for the event.

**(a)** Choose a suitable date – the first Monday of next month. Enter the details in the electronic diary and print one copy in weekly view.

**(b)** Use the Internet to find a suitable venue in Dumbarton. You require the following:

- a suitable room (to be priced between £75 and £100) for use all day
- five tables (seating four delegates each)
- a digital projector and screen
- catering: to include tea/coffee on arrival, mid-morning and mid-afternoon, and a three-course lunch
- each table of delegates should be provided with one bottle of still water and one bottle of sparkling water

**(c)** Use this information to complete the spreadsheet. Print one copy showing figures and one copy showing formulae.

**(d)** Edit the letter template to create a letter to send to the chosen hotel confirming the booking/requirements for the training day. Print one copy.

**(e)** Create a notice to be posted on the noticeboard/intranet reminding all admin assistants about the training day. Print one copy.

**(f)** Create a group e-mail to inform all administrative staff of the training day, informing them of the relevant information (the date and the venue, including the address and the directions/map). Each admin assistant must confirm that they will be able to attend. Print one copy.

**2.** Follow-up activities

**(a)** Prepare a feedback form to be issued to each attendee. Print one copy.

**(b)** Update the database – add a new field 'Training Day' (format as Yes/No) and complete to show that all administrative assistants attended.

**(c)** Edit the letter template to create a letter to the trainer, thanking them for their contribution to a successful event.

### Skill

- Literacy
- Numeracy
- Employability
- Skills for learning, life and work

### Activity

The monthly sales meeting will take place next week. Download the folder *Activity Files* from the Leckie & Leckie website (see page 5) and complete the following tasks.

1. Prepare the Notice of Meeting and the Agenda. Use the template and follow the instructions given in the comments. Delete the comments and print one copy of the finished document.
2. Finalise the presentation to be shown to the attendees. Load the file and follow the instructions given in the comments. Delete the comments and print one copy of the presentation in **handout format** (three slides to a page).
3. Complete the Minutes from the last meeting for signature by the Chairperson. Load the file and follow the instructions given in the comments. Delete the comments and print one copy of the finished document.
4. Prepare a notice to be placed on the door – *Meeting in progress*.

## Summary

An event is an important, planned occasion such as a meeting, training event, sales conference, etc. To ensure the success of an event, an admin assistant will be required to carry out tasks before, on the day of and after the event.

***Before the event***

A to-do list or a priorities list will be prepared by the admin assistant with a list of all tasks to be undertaken in relation to the event.

- A suitable date should be selected and entered into the relevant people's (electronic) diaries.
- A venue should then be chosen and booked. The admin assistant should give careful consideration to the venue to ensure it is appropriate.
- A spreadsheet is a useful tool for ensuring the event keeps within the budget originally set.
- Invitations should be sent to key/guest speakers.
- If the event is a meeting, an agenda and notice of meeting will be sent to those eligible to attend.
- Often the event needs to be advertised: promotional materials should be prepared and distributed.

- A database should be created with details of all attendees – this could be used to produce name badges and place cards. A room plan should also be created.
- The admin assistant may also be responsible for preparing a presentation for the guest speaker using presentation software.
- If attendees are to receive information at the event, the admin assistant should ensure that an attendee pack is prepared.

*On the day of the event*

- The admin assistant is responsible for ensuring all relevant documentation is available, for example attendee packs, presentation for guest/key speaker, etc.
- The room should be set out as per the room plan and direction signs should placed in appropriate areas.
- Attendance at the event should be recorded – this can be done using the database prepared at the planning stage.
- Catering arrangements should be checked.
- During the event the admin assistant should assist guest speakers and attendees with any questions/queries.
- If the event is a meeting the admin assistant will be required to take minutes of the meeting.

*Follow-up tasks*

- The room should be cleared and tidied up.
- Evaluation forms should be prepared and sent to attendees to gather feedback on the event. These forms should be reviewed and suggestions should be considered when planning future events.
- Management may require a brief report on the event.
- If the event was a meeting the admin assistant should prepare the Minutes of Meeting and send them to the Chairperson. Action Minutes may also be prepared.
- Thank you letters should be sent to the venue and to guest speakers.
- The attendee database should be checked to ensure it has been updated with the actual people who were present at the event.
- The budget spreadsheet should also be updated with actual costs of the event and a comparison made of actual and budgeted costs.
- Information about a successful event may be placed on the organisation's website or social media.

## Learning Checklist

| Skills, knowledge and understanding | Strength ☺ | 😐 | Weakness ☹ | Next steps |
|---|---|---|---|---|
| I understand what an event is. | | | | |
| I understand the tasks undertaken by an admin assistant when planning for the event. | | | | |
| I understand the tasks undertaken by an admin assistant on the day of the event. | | | | |
| I understand the tasks undertaken by an admin assistant following the event. | | | | |

Season 1
Season 2
Season 3
Season 4
2007
2008
2009
2010
2011
2012

# 2

# IT Solutions for Administrators

# 6 Word processing

**You should already know**

- I can approach familiar and new situations with confidence when selecting and using appropriate software to solve increasingly complex problems or issues. **TCH 4-03a**
- I can use ICT effectively in different learning contexts across the curriculum to access, select and present relevant information in a range of tasks. **TCH 4-03b**
- Throughout my learning, I can make effective use of a computer system to process and organise information. **TCH 4-04a**
- To facilitate the transfer of skills between classroom and the world of work, I can select and use specialist equipment and appropriate software to develop administrative and management skills. **TCH 4-06a**
- Whilst working in a simulated or real workplace, I can select and use appropriate software to carry out a range of tasks which support business and entrepreneurial activities. **TCH 4-07a**

**In this chapter you will learn about**

- Formatting functions required in word processing for National 4 and 5 Administration and IT.
- Formatting functions that can be used when creating forms.
- Business documents you may be asked to prepare.

## What should I be able to do?

**Watch point**

Word processing is a skill. It can take time to develop this skill. Practice is very important.

An admin assistant will support the work of the organisation by providing word processing support. This includes keying in (preparing), editing and updating a variety of documents.

Any documents that are word processed bythe admin assistant must be accurate and contain no spelling or grammatical errors. It could harm the reputation of an efficient organisation if documents are sent to customers that are not presented to a professional standard. It is therefore very important that the admin assistant takes time to check over the work – this is known as proofreading. While the spell check and grammar check functions of the software are very useful and should be used, they should never be used as an alternative to proofreading all documents.

## Quick-look list

The word processing skills shown below are required for this course. National 5 pupils should be able to perform skills at both National 4 and National 5 levels.

| Skill | Shown on page: |
|---|---|
| **Formatting** | |
| • Select and change font, font size | 66 |
| • Set and change margins | 67 |
| • Carry out manuscript corrections | 67 |
| • Use bold, italics and underline | 68 |
| • Align text | 68 |
| • Change line spacing | 68 |
| • Insert graphic | 68 |
| • Use bullets and numbering | 68 |
| • Insert headers and footers | 69 |
| • Borders and shading | 69 |
| • Page numbering | 69 |
| • Insert text, delete text, move text | 69 |
| **Create a simple table** | |
| • Insert, delete or amend data | 70 |
| • Add or delete rows | 70 |
| • Add or delete columns | 70 |
| • Change column widths | 70 |
| • Include/remove borders | 70 |
| • Insert shading within cells | 70 |
| • Sort data | 70 |
| • Merge cells | 71 |
| • Rotate text within cells | 71 |
| • Formulae | 71 |
| **Printing** | |
| • Completed document | 71 |
| • Specific pages | 71 |
| • Documents showing merge fields | 71 |

You may be asked to prepare a variety of business documents including:

- letters (application, thank you, enquiry)
- forms, such as a travel booking form
- itinerary
- agenda

- personal CV
- reports on research findings
- address labels
- reports
- name badges
- forms
- certificates

**Watch point**

You should become familiar with your school's house style and use it when preparing documents.

Look at documents that are produced by your school office, for example letters to parents. Is the same layout always used?

## House style

In order that all documents that originate from the same organisation look similar, a house style is used. This ensures that all staff use the same layouts when completing documents. There may be a house style book for staff can refer to, or documents may be stored as templates on the organisation's intranet for staff to access. The use of house style documents will enhance the organisation's corporate image.

## Who uses word processing in an organisation?

| Department | Use of word processing |
|---|---|
| Human Resources/Personnel Department | Key in letters to (un)successful job applicants. |
| Sales Department | Key in quotations and price lists. |
| Purchases Department | Key in letters of enquiry. |

An admin assistant working in any department may be regularly asked to prepare/edit word processed documents or forms.

## Formatting

### *Select and change font, font size*

To emphasise a relevant section of work or perhaps when preparing headed paper or a notice, you may be required to change the font (how the text looks).

Always consider how your finished document will look – too many changes of font can be distracting and will not enhance your document.

You may also be asked to increase or decrease the size of font, for example from 10 pt to 12 pt.

- This font is 11 pt Calibri.
- This font is 18 pt Kristen ITC.

> **Watch point**
> If you are asked to increase or decrease the size of font, ensure that you make it obvious you have done so, for example increase the font from 10 pt to 18 pt.

*Set and change margins*

A default margin is set when you open a new document. You may be instructed to change the default.

> **Watch point**
> Margins are shown on the left/right and top/bottom of the document. Ensure that you read instructions carefully and change the appropriate margins.

*Carry-out manuscript corrections*

Once a document has been printed it should be given a final check. If any changes are to be made to the printed document they should be made using manuscript correction signs.

## Manuscript correction signs

| Margin sign | Text sign | Meaning |
|---|---|---|
| l.c. | conFerence | Lower case letter |
| NP | [The long winding... | New paragraph |
| run on | ...at last. Then the traffic... | No new paragraph – carry stright on |
| stet | regardless | Do not delete – the word with a broken line underneath goes back in |
| u/l | The newset recruit | Underlin text |
| trs | white and black | Transpose words (or characters) |
| CAPS | School | Captial letters |
| u.c. | johnSmith | Captial or upper case letter |
| close up | Edin burgh | Close up space |
| del | The ugly duckling | Delete letter or word |
| quick | The brown fox | Insert letter or word |
| \|—\| | | Insert a dash |
| \|-\| | | Insert a hyphen |
| black | | Make word clearer |
| ⊙ | The end of the sentence | Insert a full stop |

### *Use bold, italics and underline*

These formats can be used to make relevant or important text more obvious or to enhance the overall document. Ensure that these enhancements are used thoughtfully and consider how the finished document will look – is the **relevant** *information* <u>obvious</u>?

### *Align text*

The default for text is left aligned – this means all text starts at the same point on the left-hand side of the page. However, text can also be centred in the middle of the document, right aligned (all text starts at the right hand side of the page) or justified (all text starts at the same point and ends at the same point – like the pages of this book!

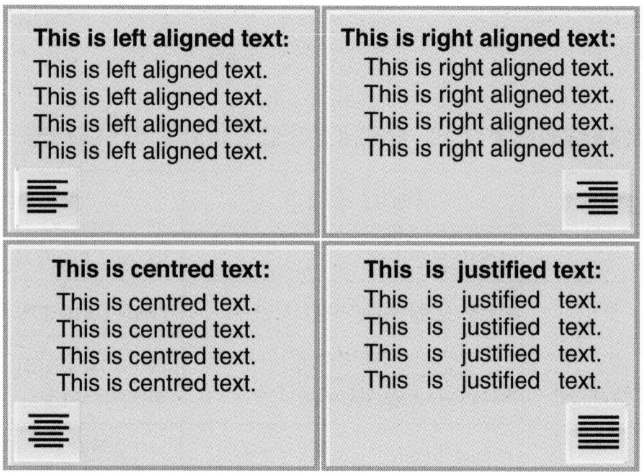


### *Change line spacing*

Line spacing can be single, 1.5 or double. You may be asked to select the whole document to change the line spacing, or to only change selected text, for example one paragraph. You must highlight the text to be changed before performing the line spacing function.

### *Insert graphic*

Graphics can be used to enhance your document. However, always make sure that any graphic is relevant to the content of the document.

**Watch point**

Ensure that all of the graphic is visible – that it is not clipped. Also, graphics should not cover any text.

### *Use bullets and numbering*

It is common for brief points in a list to be bulleted or numbered. It draws the attention of the reader to important information. Different styles of bullets are available – choose which one you prefer and stick to it, this ensures consistency within the document.

- These are some of the styles of bullets you can use.
- These are some of the styles of bullets you can use.
- These are some of the styles of bullets you can use.
- These are some of the styles of bullets you can use.
- These are some of the styles of bullets you can use.

### *Insert headers and footers*

Headers and footers are used to display additional information, for example chapter headings or a slogan.

### *Borders and shading*

Borders and shading are another method of emphasising text within a document. Borders can be placed around certain information in the document or around the whole page. In this book, National 5 information has been shaded to make it distinctive from National 4 information.

> **Watch point**
> When using shading ensure that all text can still be clearly seen.

### *Page numbering*

If a document has a few pages it may be a good idea to number them so that if they get mixed up it is easy for the reader to identify which page comes next. Page numbers have many different styles and can be placed in the header or footer.

> **Watch point**
> You may be asked to only include page numbers on certain pages of your document. Ensure you know how to do this.

### *Insert text, delete text, move text*

You may be asked to insert additional text. If doing this you must ensure that all line spacing remains consistent. Text may be deleted by highlighting it and pressing the **backspace** or **delete** key. To move text, the **cut and paste** function can be used – always double check that all text to be moved has been selected before selecting 'cut'. The spacing between paragraphs should always be checked once a cut and paste is completed.

> **Watch point**
> Save your work on a regular basis. If the work you are completing is important you should back-up your file. This means taking a second copy and storing it in a separate location.

## Creating tables

Tables can be used to present information more clearly for the user.

You may have a word processing checklist that you use to evaluate your progress through this section of the course. This will probably have been created using a table.

Column

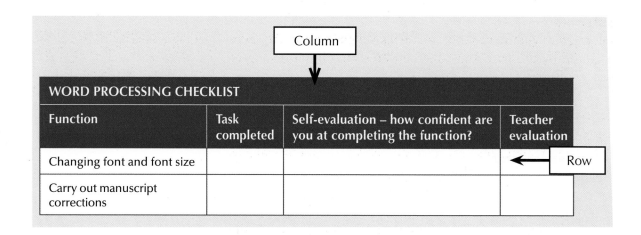

| WORD PROCESSING CHECKLIST | | | |
|---|---|---|---|
| **Function** | **Task completed** | **Self-evaluation – how confident are you at completing the function?** | **Teacher evaluation** |
| Changing font and font size | | | |
| Carry out manuscript corrections | | | |

Row

> **Watch point**
>
> There are many different formats that can be used when preparing a table. Take time to experiment with some!

***Add or delete rows***

Rows can be added easily at the bottom of the table. However, read all instructions carefully and if the row has to be inserted into the middle of the table ensure you follow the instructions for your software. To delete a row in a table, highlight the row and follow the instructions specific to your software – ensure lines in the table are also deleted.

***Add or delete columns***

Columns can be inserted at any point in the table. They can also be deleted if they are no longer required. Follow instructions specific to your software to do this.

***Change column widths***

Information should be clearly displayed within the table. Always check that words are not split over two lines; if this is the case then expand the column width. Similarly, if the default column width is too wide for the information contained in the column, then reduce it.

***Include/remove borders***

When a table is displayed, borders are shown around each 'cell' (or box). These can be removed – either around the whole table or around specific boxes.

***Insert shading within cells***

Shading can be used to emphasise information contained within the table. In the example shown on page 71 the total amount due has been shaded.

***Sort data***

Information within the table can be displayed in a specific order required by the user. The table can be sorted in ascending or descending order per column.

**Watch point**

Ascending = A–Z (going up). Descending = Z–A (going down).

***Merge cells and rotate cells***

Information can be displayed over two columns or rows using the merge facility. Text can also be shown at different angles within a cell, i.e. rotated.

***Formulae***

You can perform calculations within a table – this is useful if the information is contained in your word-processed document and not in a spreadsheet. Simple calculations such as SUM and AVERAGE can be calculated in a table.

Example of a table that has been formatted.

| Order Form | | | | |
|---|---|---|---|---|
| To | EVA GAMES Ltd<br>27 Glen Road<br>INVERNESS<br>IV6 7YH | | | |
| REF NO | QUANTITY | DESCRIPTION | UNIT PRICE | TOTAL PRICE |
| EG125 | 4 | Connect 4 | £5.99 | £24.95 |
| EG352 | 10 | Snakes and Ladders | £3.99 | £39.99 |
| | | | | |
| | | TOTAL AMOUNT DUE | | £59.94 |

Order Form has been merged and centred over five columns.

Borders have been removed from this section as these columns are not required.

This text is wrapped to ensure it fits into one cell

Shading has been used to highlight the total amount due – an important figure!

The formula function has been used to calculate the total amount due.

## Printing

You should be able to print the completed document, specific pages of the document and documents showing merge fields.

**Watch point**

You should find the house style layout for business documents in your school's/centre's house style booklet.

**Make the Link**

- You may be asked to word process in many different subjects within the school. It is useful to word process projects like essays as they can be drafted and edited easily – meaning you do not need to continually re-write them.
- Word processing is a very useful skill that you can make use of while at school and beyond.

## Business documents you may be asked to prepare

| Document | Use |
|---|---|
| Letter | A formal document that is sent to customers, suppliers etc.<br>• Should be prepared using the organisation's headed paper and should always include a reference, date, inside address, salutation and complementary close. |
| Forms | For example, travel booking forms, accident report forms.<br>• Often prepared using a table.<br>• Always ensure that appropriate space is left between sections, particularly if the form is to be completed manually. |
| Itinerary | Prepared for someone who is going on a business trip.<br>• Will provide information such as who is going on the trip, dates of the trip, transport details (times and places of departure/arrival), meetings (times and place), accommodation details etc.<br>• Often prepared using a table. |
| Agenda | Prepared and sent out to people who will be attending a meeting.<br>• Will provide information on what is to be discussed at a meeting and the order in which the discussion will take place. |
| Curriculum Vitae | Prepared by a job applicant.<br>• Will give information on the candidate, such as contact details, qualifications, employment history and other information in support of the application. |
| Report on research findings | A formal document that should contain a heading, introduction, main findings and summary. |
| Address labels | The address of a customer/supplier etc can be printed onto a label and placed on an envelope.<br>• Less time-consuming than writing out addresses. |
| Name badges | Name badges may be required by attendees at an event.<br>• Printing name badges gives them a professional look. |
| Certificates | Certificates to celebrate success, such as good employee attendance.<br>• Can be prepared to a high standard. |

## Activity

The following document has been checked for errors after being printed.

*ADMINISTRATIVE ASSISTANT*

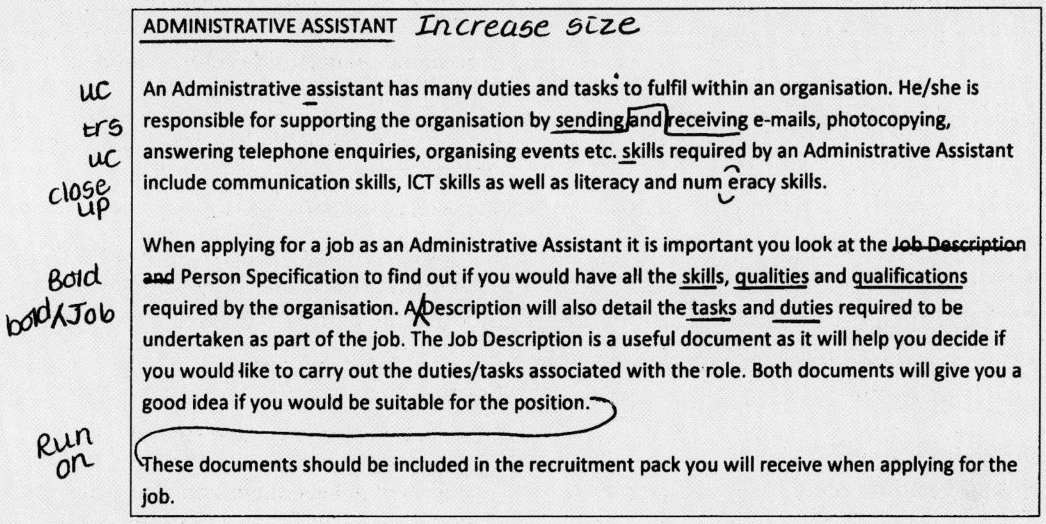

ADMINISTRATIVE ASSISTANT Increase size

uc / trs / uc / close up — An Administrative assistant has many duties and tasks to fulfil within an organisation. He/she is responsible for supporting the organisation by sending and receiving e-mails, photocopying, answering telephone enquiries, organising events etc. skills required by an Administrative Assistant include communication skills, ICT skills as well as literacy and num eracy skills.

Bold / bold ^Job — When applying for a job as an Administrative Assistant it is important you look at the ~~Job Description and~~ Person Specification to find out if you would have all the skills, qualities and qualifications required by the organisation. A Description will also detail the tasks and duties required to be undertaken as part of the job. The Job Description is a useful document as it will help you decide if you would like to carry out the duties/tasks associated with the role. Both documents will give you a good idea if you would be suitable for the position.

Run on — These documents should be included in the recruitment pack you will receive when applying for the job.

Download the file *Administrative Assistant* from the Leckie & Leckie website (see page 5).

1. Make the changes shown above.
2. Print one copy of the document.

## Activity

Download the file *Healthy Eating* from the Leckie & Leckie website (see page 5) and make the amendments shown below.

1. Change the font and increase the size of the main heading.
2. Change the margins to 4 cm/1.58″.
3. Embolden all shoulder headings.
4. Insert the following text as a third paragraph in the 'Iron deficiency' section:

   In contrast, tannins found in tea reduce the absorption of iron, so it's better to have a glass of orange juice with your breakfast cereal rather than a cup of tea.
5. Move the section (including the heading) headed 'Vegetarianism' to below the section 'Calcium Deficiency'.
6. In the 'Foods to Choose' section, italicise all the recommendations for teenagers – starting from 'Plenty of starchy carbohydrates' and ending with 'Take regular exercise'.
7. Embolden and underline the section on acne.
8. Bullet point all information in the 'Key Points' section.
9. Insert an appropriate graphic.
10. Justify the document.
11. Insert your name and school in a header.
12. Insert the page numbers in the footer and right align them.
13. Print one copy of the document.

## Activity

Borders Community Group is to host a Book Fair in Hawick Town Hall. You have been asked to complete a letter. Download the file *Book Fair* from the Leckie & Leckie website (see page 5).

1. Insert a suitable reference and date.
2. Action and delete the comments within the file.
3. Include the following as the third paragraph:

   We are always keen to use the Town Hall for the benefit of our local community. If you have any ideas for events that you feel may encourage community spirit please contact me on 01450 567149.
4. Insert another row in the table and insert the following information (at the appropriate point):

   Mhairi Greenhorn. 11.45 am. Writing master class.
5. Save and print one copy of the letter.

## ★ Key questions

Central High School is having an S1 Sports Day on the first Monday in June. You have been asked to prepare a leaflet for participants.

1. Use varied formats to enhance this four-page document, which should be produced on one sheet of A4.
2. The front page should contain the name of the school, an appropriate heading, the date of the sports day and a suitable graphic.
3. The back page should contain a best wishes/good luck message and graphic.
4. Number pages 2–4 only.
5. Text for pages 2 and 3 is shown below.
6. Save and print one copy of the leaflet.

100 m race (girls): 9.30 am

| Lane | Name | Class |
|---|---|---|
| 1 | Megan McDonnell | 1C1 |
| 2 | Niamh Hughes | 1D2 |
| 3 | Dana Jones | 1A1 |
| 4 | Lara McInally | 1B2 |
| 5 | Anastasia Peel | 1C1 |
| 6 | Joanne Moffat | 1B1 |

WINNER: ..................................................................................

100 m race (boys): 9.45 am

| Lane | Name | Class |
|---|---|---|
| 1 | Harry Punch | 1D1 |
| 2 | Cameron Smith | 1A1 |
| 3 | Aidan Connell | 1C1 |
| 4 | Declan Sweeney | 1B3 |
| 5 | Josh Neilson | 1C2 |
| 6 | Callum Connelly | 1D3 |

WINNER: ..................................................................................

### ⚠ Watch point

You could use a table here to display the information.

400 m race (girls): 9.55 am

| Lane | Name | Class |
|---|---|---|
| 1 | Erica Murray | 1C2 |
| 2 | Orla Neilson | 1A3 |
| 3 | Eva Brawley | 1D2 |
| 4 | Grace Higgins | 1A2 |
| 5 | Amy Watt | 1C3 |
| 6 | Abby Taylor | 1B1 |

WINNER: ..........................................................................

400 m race (boys): 10.10 am

| Lane | Name | Class |
|---|---|---|
| 1 | Luke McCrossan | 1C3 |
| 2 | Jack Lawlor | 1A1 |
| 3 | Antony Higgins | 1B3 |
| 4 | Christie Boyle | 1C1 |
| 5 | Christopher Peters | 1A3 |
| 6 | Harry Duffy | 1D2 |

WINNER: ..........................................................................

200 m Hurdles (girls): 10.15 am

| Lane | Name | Class |
|---|---|---|
| 1 | Holly Dolan | 1D1 |
| 2 | Chloe Pearce | 1A1 |
| 3 | Jessica Stewart | 1C3 |
| 4 | Lesley Marshall | 1B3 |
| 5 | Lynne Anderson | 1C1 |
| 6 | Maria McLeish | 1B2 |

WINNER: ..........................................................................

400 m Hurdles (boys): 10.30 am

| Lane | Name | Class |
|---|---|---|
| 1 | Alex Nicol | 1C1 |
| 2 | Robert McDonald | 1A1 |
| 3 | Christopher Philbin | 1D2 |
| 4 | Clinton Boyd | 1D1 |
| 5 | Kevin McPherson | 1C2 |
| 6 | Finlay Donald | 1D3 |

WINNER: ..........................................................................

Hockey Finals: 1 pm (Pitch 1)

1C1 v 1D2

WINNER: ..........................................................................

Football finals: Kick-off 1 pm (Pitch 2)

1A1 v 1D3

WINNER: ..........................................................................

## Skill

- ICT skills
- Literacy
- Numeracy
- Employability
- Skills for learning, life and work

## Activity

***Activity 1: individually or pairs***

**1.** Research a pop group/singer of your choice. You should find out the following:
- Names of five of their top 40 hits.
- The position each reached in the charts.
- Number of downloads (records sold) for each top 40 hit.

**2.** Enter the information into a table and then attempt the following tasks:

**(a)** Ensure the heading for your table is **merged** over three columns and **centred**.

**(b)** Rotate headings – you can choose your preferred text direction.

**(c)** Sort the information into ascending order of number of records sold.

**(d)** Enter a row at the bottom of the table and label it 'Total number of records sold'.

**(e)** Enter a formula to calculate the total number of records sold'.

**(f)** Border and shade the cell that contains the Total number of records sold' figure.

(*continued*)

***Activity 2: individually or pairs***

1. Find out information on the top goal scorers for Scotland's national football team. Create a table that contains the following information:
   - name of scorer
   - club football team (at the time of scoring)
   - number of goals scored
2. Enter the information into a table and then attempt the following tasks:
   **(a)** Ensure the heading for your table is merged over three columns and centred.
   **(b)** Rotate headings – you can choose your preferred text direction.
   **(c)** Sort the information into ascending order of number of goals scored.
   **(d)** Enter a row at the bottom of the table and label it 'Total number of goals scored'.
   **(e)** Enter a formula to calculate the number of goals scored.
   **(f)** Border and shade the cell that contains the name of the person who scored the most goals.

## Summary

In this topic you have learned what is expected of you at both National 4 and National 5 levels, i.e. the skills you should be able to carry out at each level.

- You have learned what is meant by a variety of formatting terms associated with word processing, and in particular creating forms.
- By carrying out the tasks, key question and questions you will have practised the skills required for National 4 and National 5 Administration and IT.

## Learning Checklist

| | Skills, knowledge and understanding | Strength ☺ | 😐 | Weakness ☹ | Next steps |
|---|---|---|---|---|---|
| Formatting | **Formatting**<br>I can select and change font, font size | | | | • Refer to instructions<br>• Complete additional tasks<br>• Ask teacher for help |
| | I can set and change margins | | | | • Refer to instructions<br>• Complete additional tasks<br>• Ask teacher for help |
| | I can carry out manuscript corrections | | | | • Refer to instructions<br>• Complete additional tasks<br>• Ask teacher for help |
| | I can use bold, italics and underline | | | | • Refer to instructions<br>• Complete additional tasks<br>• Ask teacher for help |
| | I can align text | | | | • Refer to instructions<br>• Complete additional tasks<br>• Ask teacher for help |
| | I can change line spacing | | | | • Refer to instructions<br>• Complete additional tasks<br>• Ask teacher for help |
| | I can insert a graphic | | | | • Refer to instructions<br>• Complete additional tasks<br>• Ask teacher for help |
| | I can use bullets and numbering | | | | • Refer to instructions<br>• Complete additional tasks<br>• Ask teacher for help |
| | I can insert headers and footers | | | | • Refer to instructions<br>• Complete additional tasks<br>• Ask teacher for help |
| | I can insert borders and shading | | | | • Refer to instructions<br>• Complete additional tasks<br>• Ask teacher for help |
| | I can insert page numbering | | | | • Refer to instructions<br>• Complete additional tasks<br>• Ask teacher for help |
| | I can insert, delete and move text | | | | • Refer to instructions<br>• Complete additional tasks<br>• Ask teacher for help |

(*continued*)

| | Skills, knowledge and understanding | Strength ☺ | 😐 | Weakness ☹ | Next steps |
|---|---|---|---|---|---|
| Tables | I can insert, delete or amend data | | | | • Refer to instructions<br>• Complete additional tasks<br>• Ask teacher for help |
| | I can add or delete rows | | | | • Refer to instructions<br>• Complete additional tasks<br>• Ask teacher for help |
| | I can add of delete columns | | | | • Refer to instructions<br>• Complete additional tasks<br>• Ask teacher for help |
| | I can change column widths | | | | • Refer to instructions<br>• Complete additional tasks<br>• Ask teacher for help |
| | I can include/remove borders | | | | • Refer to instructions<br>• Complete additional tasks<br>• Ask teacher for help |
| | I can insert shading within cells | | | | • Refer to instructions<br>• Complete additional tasks<br>• Ask teacher for help |
| | I can sort data | | | | • Refer to instructions<br>• Complete additional tasks<br>• Ask teacher for help |
| | I can merge cells | | | | • Refer to instructions<br>• Complete additional tasks<br>• Ask teacher for help |
| | I can rotate text within cells | | | | • Refer to instructions<br>• Complete additional tasks<br>• Ask teacher for help |
| | I can insert formulae | | | | • Refer to instructions<br>• Complete additional tasks<br>• Ask teacher for help |
| Printing | I can print completed documents | | | | • Refer to instructions<br>• Complete additional tasks<br>• Ask teacher for help |
| | I can print specific pages | | | | • Refer to instructions<br>• Complete additional tasks<br>• Ask teacher for help |
| | I can print documents showing merge fields | | | | • Refer to instructions<br>• Complete additional tasks<br>• Ask teacher for help |

| | Skills, knowledge and understanding | Strength ☺ | 😐 | Weakness ☹ | Next steps |
|---|---|---|---|---|---|
| Documents | I can prepare letters (application, thank you, enquiry) | | | | • Refer to instructions<br>• Complete additional tasks<br>• Ask teacher for help |
| | I can prepare forms eg travel booking form | | | | • Refer to instructions<br>• Complete additional tasks<br>• Ask teacher for help |
| | I can prepare an itinerary | | | | • Refer to instructions<br>• Complete additional tasks<br>• Ask teacher for help |
| | I can prepare an agenda | | | | • Refer to instructions<br>• Complete additional tasks<br>• Ask teacher for help |
| | I can prepare a personal CV | | | | • Refer to instructions<br>• Complete additional tasks<br>• Ask teacher for help |
| | I can prepare reports on research findings | | | | • Refer to instructions<br>• Complete additional tasks<br>• Ask teacher for help |
| | I can prepare address labels | | | | • Refer to instructions<br>• Complete additional tasks<br>• Ask teacher for help |
| | I can prepare reports | | | | • Refer to instructions<br>• Complete additional tasks<br>• Ask teacher for help |
| | I can prepare name badges | | | | • Refer to instructions<br>• Complete additional tasks<br>• Ask teacher for help |
| | I can prepare forms | | | | • Refer to instructions<br>• Complete additional tasks<br>• Ask teacher for help |
| | I can prepare certificates | | | | • Refer to instructions<br>• Complete additional tasks<br>• Ask teacher for help |

# 7 Spreadsheets

**You should already know**

- I can approach familiar and new situations with confidence when selecting and using appropriate software to solve increasingly complex problems or issues. **TCH 4-03a**
- I can use ICT effectively in different learning contexts across the curriculum to access, select and present relevant information in a range of tasks. **TCH 4-03b**
- To facilitate the transfer of skills between classroom and the world of work, I can select and use specialist equipment and appropriate software to develop administrative and management skills. **TCH 4-06a**
- Whilst working in a simulated or real workplace, I can select and use appropriate software to carry out a range of tasks which support business and entrepreneurial activities. **TCH 4-07a**
- I can evaluate and interpret raw and graphical data using a variety of methods, comment on relationships I observe within the data and communicate my findings to others. **MNU 4-20a**

**In this chapter you will learn about:**

- The tasks you should be able to perform using a spreadsheet package.
- The purpose of a spreadsheet.
- The use of a spreadsheet package by different departments in an organisation.
- The advantages of using a spreadsheet.
- Formatting cells.
- Formulae, functions and features.
- Editing a spreadsheet.
- Creating charts.
- Printing (extracts of) worksheets.

## What should I be able to do?

This part of the course requires you to solve business problems and present the solution using a spreadsheet. The skills needed at both levels are shown below. National 5 pupils should be able to perform skills at both National 4 and National 5 levels.

## Quick-look list

If you want to quickly check what spreadsheet tasks you should be able to perform, refer to the list shown below.

| Skill | Shown on page: |
|---|---|
| **Formatting** | |
| • Text alignment | 86 |
| • Borders and shading | 86 |
| • Different fonts, styles, sizes | 86 |
| • Currency, date, number to specified decimal places, percentages | 86 |
| **Formulae, functions and features** | |
| • Basic arithmetic formulae | 87 |
| • Average | 88 |
| • Maximum | 88 |
| • Minimum | 88 |
| • Count | 88 |
| • IF | 88 |
| • Conditional formatting | 88 |
| • Link cells within worksheets | 89 |
| • Use named cells | 89 |
| • Relative and absolute cell references | 89 |
| **Editing a spreadsheet** | |
| • Input and edit data | 89 |
| • Sort data | 90 |
| • Insert/delete columns/rows | 90 |
| **Creating a simple chart from a specified range** | |
| • Pie chart | 90 |
| • Bar or column chart | 91 |
| • Line graph | 91 |
| • Labelling charts, including the use of data labels | 91 |
| **Creating a chart and labelling it independently using data from adjacent and non-adjacent cells** | |
| • Pie chart; bar or column chart; line graph | 92 |
| • Labelling charts meaningfully, including the use of data labels | 92 |
| **Printing worksheets** | |
| • Showing value view | 92 |
| • Showing formulae view | 92 |
| • With and without gridlines | 92 |
| • With and without row and column headings | 92 |
| • In portrait and landscape orientation | 92 |
| • With headers and footers | 92 |
| • To fit on one page | 92 |
| **Printing worksheets and extracts of worksheets** | |
| • Showing value/formulae view | 92 |
| • With or without gridlines or row/column headings | 92 |
| • In portrait/landscape orientation | 92 |
| • With headers/footers | 92 |
| • To fit on one page | 92 |

## What is a spreadsheet?

- A spreadsheet is a computer program designed to display and process numbers.
- It is a grid that is made up of cells, identified by column letters and row numbers.
- Each cell can contain text, numbers or formulae (to carry out calculations).

For example:

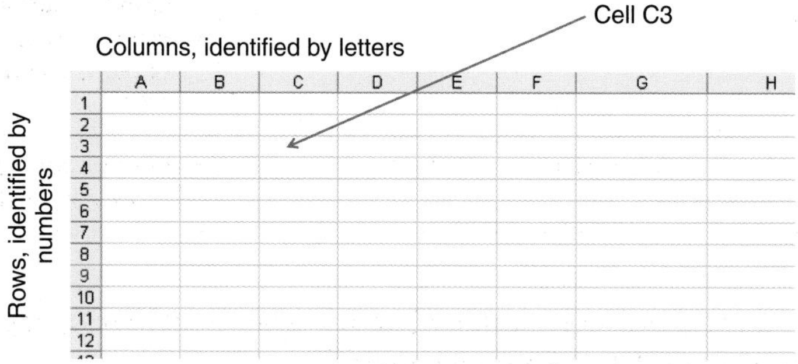


- A spreadsheet is a powerful tool for carrying out calculations and testing different mathematical possibilities.
- Simple calculations can be carried out, for example add (+), subtract (–), multiply (*) and divide (/).

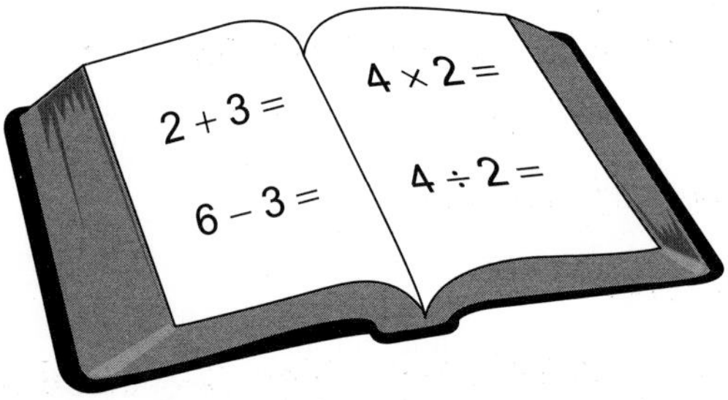


- More complex calculations can be carried out by using a range of built-in functions, for example add a range of cells (SUM), find the average (AVERAGE), find the highest number (MAX), etc.

You will learn more about calculations and functions later in this chapter.

## Who uses spreadsheets in an organisation?

| Department | Use of spreadsheets |
|---|---|
| Human Resources/Personnel Department | • Record employees' absences/holidays.<br>• Calculate training costs. |
| Finance Department | • Calculate employee wages.<br>• Calculate the profit/loss of the organisation.<br>• Prepare departmental budgets. |
| Sales Department | • Calculate sales figures.<br>• Create charts/graphs to help analyse sales figures.<br>• Prepare 'what if?' scenarios, such as 'what would be the effect on a company's profit if we reduced prices by 4%?' |
| Purchases Department | • Record issue and receipt of stock.<br>• Complete order forms. |

An admin assistant working in any department may be regularly asked to update data on a spreadsheet.

## Advantages of using spreadsheets

- present your data effectively by using formatting features
- calculate and recalculate quickly and accurately using formulae
- replicate formulae saving time, reducing errors
- sort data
- carry out 'what if?' scenarios
- display data graphically

## Formatting

Formatting means changing the way in which the information is displayed (for example, text alignment, borders and shading, font, size, style) or setting up a cell to contain numbers in a particular format (for example, £, %, date, decimal places).

***Text alignment***

Text can be aligned horizontally, for example:

| | | |
|---|---|---|
| Left | Centre | Right |

When using a spreadsheet package, text is automatically left aligned and numbers/values are automatically right aligned.

Or, text can be wrapped, to be shown over more than one line within a cell, and also aligned horizontally, for example:

| | | |
|---|---|---|
| This text is wrapped and left aligned | This text is wrapped and centre aligned | This text is wrapped and right aligned |

Wrapping text is useful for when inserting a long column heading.

***Borders and shading***

A cell can have a border or shading applied to make it stand out, for example:

| | |
|---|---|
| This information stands out because of the border | This information stands out because of the shading |

***Different fonts, styles, sizes***

Cells can also be formatted for appearance, for example to show the contents as a specified size, in bold, underlined, or italicised.

| | | | |
|---|---|---|---|
| Size | **Bold** | Underline | *Italics* |

Formatting in this way helps identify information that is important, for example headings.

***Formatting cells to currency, percentage, date, decimal places***

A cell can be formatted to show any number entered to appear automatically with £, %, with a specified number of decimal places or in a particular date format. For example:

| | |
|---|---|
| Format number to show percentage | 10% |
| Format number to show currency | £10.25 |
| Format number to show specified number of decimal places, eg 2 | 7.50 |

## Formulae, functions and features

All formulae must start with '=' to tell the computer to carry out the calculation.

***Basic arithmetic formulae***

This type of formula uses only two cell references.

**Watch point**

You should never key in the cell reference but use the mouse to click on the cell and the computer will enter the appropriate cell reference for you.

| Arithmetic calculation<br>➔ *Real-world example* | Arithmetic symbol/ function | Formula (explanation) |
|---|---|---|
| Add two numbers<br>➔ *Calculate the total of two numbers* | + | = A1 + A2<br>(contents of cell A1 added to contents of cell A2) |
| Subtract one number from another<br>➔ *Calculate the difference between two numbers* | – | = A1 – A2<br>(contents of cell A2 subtracted from contents of cell A1) |
| Multiply one number by another<br>➔ *Calculate the total cost where you have cost per item and quantity* | * | = A1 – A2<br>(contents of cell A1 multiplied by contents of cell A2) |
| Divide one number by another<br>➔ *Calculate the percentage of items sold, for example the total of item 1 as a percentage of overall total sold* | / | = A1 / A2<br>(contents of cell A1 divided by contents of cell A2) |

When adding more than two cells you should use the SUM function (Σ).

| Arithmetic calculation<br>➔ *Real-world example* | Arithmetic symbol/function | Formula (explanation) |
|---|---|---|
| Add several numbers<br>➔ *Calculate the total value of items sold when there are more than two items* | SUM | =SUM(A1:A10)<br>(contents of the range of cells A1 through to A10 added together) |

Functions: average, maximum, minimum, count

| **Arithmetic calculation**<br>**→ *Real-world example*** | **Arithmetic symbol/function** | **Formula (explanation)** |
|---|---|---|
| Calculate the average number<br>→ *Calculate the average cost from a list* | AVERAGE | =AVERAGE(A1:A10)<br>(the average is calculated from the contents of the range of cells A1 through to A10) |
| Identify the highest number from a list<br>→ *Identify the best-selling product from a list* | MAX | =MAX(A1:A10)<br>(the highest number is identified from the contents of the range of cells A1 through to A10) |
| Identify the lowest number from a list<br>→ *Identify the least popular product from a list* | MIN | =MIN(A1:A10)<br>(the lowest number is identified from the contents of the range of cells A1 through to A10) |
| Count the number of entries in a list<br>→ *Count the number of products available for sale* | COUNT | =COUNT(A1:A10)<br>(the number of cells containing a number is counted from the range of cells A1 through to A10) |

**Watch point**

You should never key in a formula containing functions, but use the function tool.

### *If (conditional formula)*

| | | |
|---|---|---|
| Conditional formula – follow a course of action depending on the outcome (two possibilities) | IF | =IF(A1>50,10%,0)<br>(if the contents of cell A1 is greater than 50 (true) then the value 10% will be entered, if the contents of cell A1 are not greater than 50 (false) then the value 0 will be entered) |
| A condition is set, followed by one outcome if true and an alternative outcome if false. | | =IF(A1>50,'Yes','No')<br>[two possible outcomes (yes or no), text must be inside inverted commas] |
| → *Calculate whether a 10% discount should be allowed/how much discount should be allowed if a customer spends more than £50.* | | =IF(A1>50,A1*10%,0)<br>(if the contents of cell A1 are greater than 50 (true) then the contents of cell A1 will be multiplied by 10% and this answer will be entered, if the contents of cell A1 are not greater than 50 (false) then the value 0 will be entered) |

### *Conditional formatting*

This function allows a user to change the formatting of a cell based on the value in that cell. For example, if an organisation has made a profit the value will be shown in black and if the organisation has made a loss the value will be shown in red.

***Linking cells within worksheets (working with multiple worksheets)***

It is possible to refer to a cell in another worksheet in a formula or function. When a cell is linked the formula will not only show the cell reference but also the sheet name, for example, =A1*Sheet2!A3. (The contents of cell A1 in the current worksheet will be multiplied by the contents of cell A3 in the worksheet named Sheet 2.)

***Using named cells***

It can sometimes be difficult to understand a formula using cell references. It may be less confusing to give cells meaningful names. For example =A3*VAT.

***Relative referencing***

When the same calculation is to be repeated down a column/across a row, **replication** can be used to save time and reduce errors. This is a function of a spreadsheet package that allows the same calculation to be copied down/across without having to key in the formula/function again. The cell references will change relative to the new position. For example, replicating down will change the row numbers and replicating across will change the column letters.

| |
|---|
| =A1*B1 |
| =A2*B2 |
| =A3*B3 |
| =A4*B4 |
| =A5*B5 |

**Watch point**

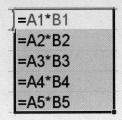

You should replicate formulae when repeating the same calculation, as this will save time and reduce errors.

***Absolute referencing***

If a cell has been set up as an absolute reference in a formula (for example, $A$1) then this cell reference will not change during replication. The $ sign in front of the column and the $ sign in front of the row number tells the computer not to change it. To make a cell reference absolute the $ sign must appear in front of both the column letter and the row number.

## Editing a spreadsheet

***Inputting and editing data***

Data can be input by clicking on the appropriate cell and keying in the information. This can be **edited** by clicking on the cell to be edited and deleting the contents or amending the information by using the edit line.

### *Comments*

This is a feature in a spreadsheet package that can help you make a worksheet easier to understand by providing additional information about the data it contains. For example, you can use a **comment** as a note that provides information about data in an individual cell.

Or, a comment can be used to provide an instruction that must be carried out. If a comment has been added, a red triangle will appear at the top right corner, for example:

| | |
|---|---|
| John | Brown |
| Adam | Lang |
| Patricia | Moffat |
| Angela | Carslaw |

In order to read the comment you must move your cursor over the cell containing the comment and the instruction will appear, for example:

| | |
|---|---|
| John | Brown |
| Adam | Lang |
| Patricia | Moffat |
| Angela | Carslaw |

**User:**
**Sort the surname into alphabetical order**

Comments can be deleted once the instruction has been carried out.

### *Sorting data*

Data in a spreadsheet can be sorted using the **sort function**. Data can be sorted into ascending or descending alphabetical or numerical order. More complex sorts can also be carried out where data is sorted on more than one category.

### *Inserting/deleting columns/rows*

By highlighting a column letter or row number, additional columns or rows can be inserted or the selected ones can be deleted. Inserting columns/rows is useful if information has been omitted as it can be easily inserted into the correct position.

## Creating charts

Data in a spreadsheet can be converted into graphical form, for example pie charts, bar charts and line graphs.

This makes the information easier to read and understand and it can be read at a glance.

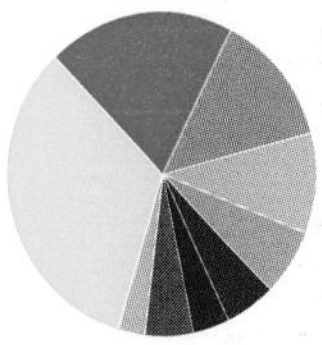

### *Pie chart*

This is used to show a **general comparison** where detail is not required. For example, to show the percentage of an organisation's spending by each department

***Bar chart***

This is used to show **comparisons** over periods of time or between different products, for example, to compare the actual and target sales figures.

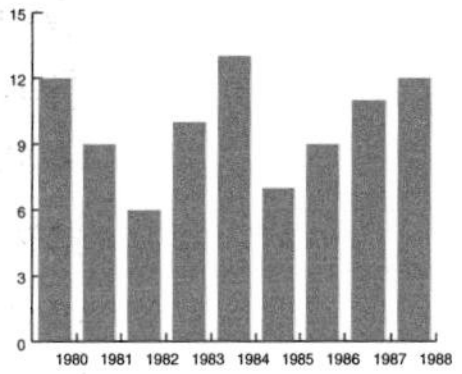


***Line graph***

This is used to show **trends** over a period of time. For example, to show how profits have risen or fallen over the last 6 months.

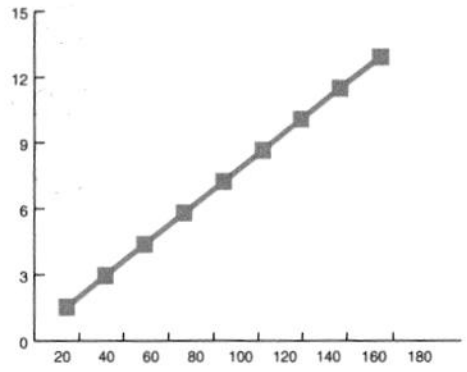


***Pictogram***

This is used to provide a **general impression** and does not provide detailed figures. For example, to show which product has had the most sales, using pictures to represent numeric information.

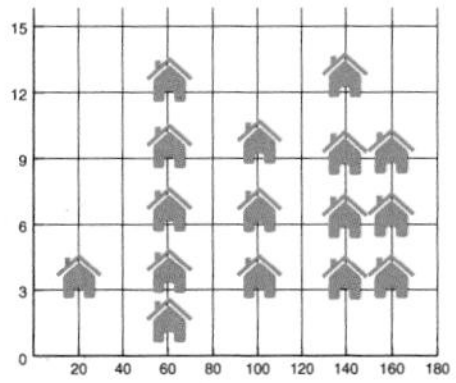


## Creating a simple chart from a specified range

A spreadsheet package may have a charting function (chart wizard), which will allow the user to select the data to be included and then take the user step-by-step through the creation of the chart. Alternatively, the user may have to build the chart using specific menus/toolbar icons.

- A chart will only be meaningful if it has been labelled appropriately.
- All charts should have a title that describes what the chart is displaying.
- Bar charts and line graphs must also have meaningful labels on the *x* and *y* axes.

**Watch point**

You should know which is the *x*-axis and which is the *y*-axis.

Charts can be printed as part of the spreadsheet or they can be printed as a separate sheet.

Before creating a chart, the user must select the information to be charted by clicking and dragging through the appropriate cells, for example from A2 to B8.

**Watch point**

Do not select totals when creating charts.

| | A | B |
|---|---|---|
| 1 | **Monthly Sales** | |
| 2 | ***Month*** | ***Sales(£000s)*** |
| 3 | Jan | 50 |
| 4 | Feb | 54 |
| 5 | Mar | 65 |
| 6 | Apr | 33 |
| 7 | May | 56 |
| 8 | Jun | 78 |
| 9 | Total | 336 |

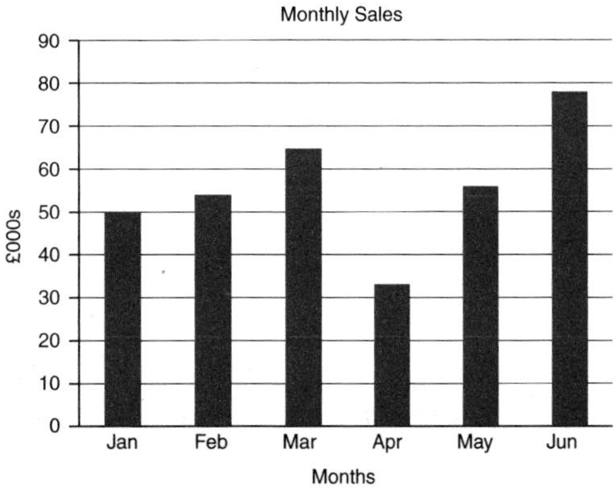

**Watch point**

When there is only a single bar in a bar/column chart, you should remove the legend. The legend is only needed when a comparison is being made.

## Creating a simple chart and labelling it using data from non-adjacent cells

Sometimes the information to be charted is not adjacent (side by side). In this instance the cells in the first column are selected first and then before clicking and dragging through the cells in the other column(s), the user must press and hold the Ctrl key.

| | A | B | C |
|---|---|---|---|
| 1 | **Monthly Sales** | | |
| 2 | ***Month*** | *Sales(£000s)* | *Target sales (£000s)* |
| 3 | Jan | 50 | 55 |
| 4 | Feb | 54 | 50 |
| 5 | Mar | 65 | 60 |
| 6 | Apr | 33 | 40 |
| 7 | May | 56 | 55 |
| 8 | Jun | 78 | 70 |
| 9 | Total | 336 | 330 |
| 10 | | | |

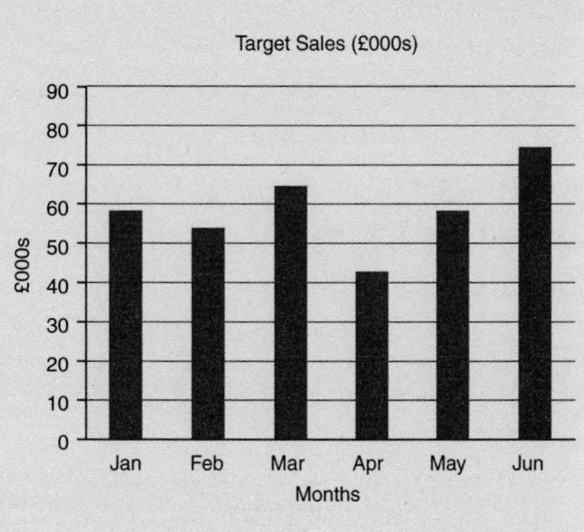


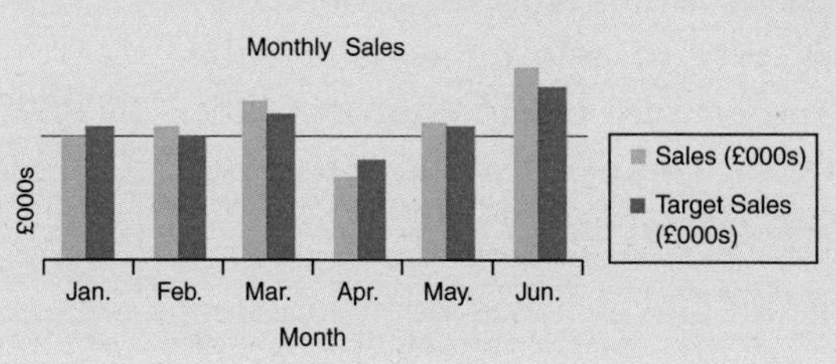

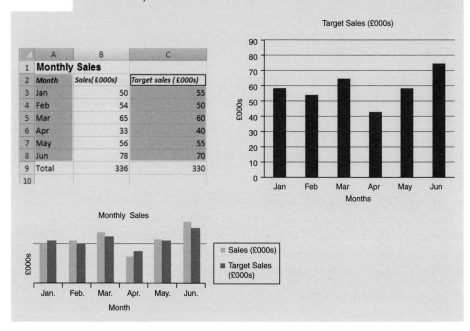

## Printing worksheets

Spreadsheets can be printed:

- to show figures
- to show formulae
- to show gridlines
- to show row/column headings
- to show headers/footers
- in portrait or landscape format
- to fit on one page

Your spreadsheet package will allow you to use appropriate menus and toolbar icons to choose how you want the printout to look.

It is also possible to print only part of a spreadsheet (known as an **extract**).

If the full spreadsheet is not to be printed then it is possible to hide the column(s)/row(s) that are not to be shown on the printout. You must then **set the print area** before printing.

**Watch point**

Always **print preview** your spreadsheet *before* sending to the printer.

**Make the Link**

- In Maths you will have carried out simple calculations and perhaps some more complex calculations. You will have charted data to make it easier to read and understand.
- In Social Studies you will have studied charts/graphs to identify trends, make comparisons.

## Activity

An organisation uses a spreadsheet to help keep track of the amount of money spent by each department each month.

| | A | B | C | D | E | F | G | H | I | J | K |
|---|---|---|---|---|---|---|---|---|---|---|---|
| 1 | **Expenditure for Jan-June** | | | | | | | | | | |
| 2 | **Department** | **Jan** | **Feb** | **Mar** | **Apr** | **May** | **Jun** | **Total** | **Average** | **Maximum** | **Minimum** |
| 3 | Human Resources | 4300 | 4352 | 3965 | 4183 | 4382 | 4171 | ? | ? | ? | ? |
| 4 | Finance | 3564 | 3627 | 3876 | 3729 | 3827 | 3827 | ? | ? | ? | ? |
| 5 | Sales | 4345 | 4352 | 4493 | 4352 | 4261 | 4162 | ? | ? | ? | ? |
| 6 | Purchases | 3750 | 4026 | 3845 | 3948 | 3827 | 3761 | ? | ? | ? | ? |
| 7 | Admin Services | 3324 | 3102 | 3293 | 3261 | 3018 | 3817 | ? | ? | ? | ? |
| 8 | **Total** | ? | ? | ? | ? | ? | ? | ? | ? | ? | ? |
| 9 | **Average** | ? | ? | ? | ? | ? | ? | ? | ? | ? | ? |
| 10 | **Maximum** | ? | ? | ? | ? | ? | ? | ? | ? | ? | ? |
| 11 | **Minimum** | ? | ? | ? | ? | ? | ? | ? | ? | ? | ? |
| 12 | | | | | | | | | | | |
| 13 | | | | | | | | | | | |
| 14 | | | | | | | | | | | |
| 15 | | | | | | | | | | | |
| 16 | | | | | | | | | | | |
| 17 | | | | | | | | | | | |

Download the file *Spreadsheet Example Task* from the Leckie & Leckie website (see page 5) and complete the following tasks.

National 5 students should carry out all the National 4 instructions as well as National 5 instructions.

| National 4 | National 5 |
|---|---|
| Align cells appropriately. | |
| | Format headings appropriately:<br>• Enlarge the size of the main heading.<br>• Use bold where appropriate. |
| Shade the department that has the highest amount of spending for the 6-month period. | |
| | Format cells as currency where appropriate |
| Use appropriate functions where you see **?** | |
| Sort the spreadsheet into alphabetical order by department. | |
| Create a bar chart to compare the spending for each department over the 6-month period. Label the chart appropriately. Print the chart. | |
| | Create a pie chart to show the total percentage of spending by each department. Label the chart appropriately. Print the chart. |
| Print one copy of the worksheet without row and column headings and with no gridlines. The printout should be on landscape orientation. Your own name and task details should be shown as a footer. | |
| Print one copy of the worksheet showing formulae, row and column headings and gridlines. The printout should be on landscape orientation. Your own name and task details should be shown as a footer. | |
| | Print one copy of an extract of the worksheet showing only the total figures for each department. |

**Watch point**

Remember to save regularly.

## Questions

1. Explain the following spreadsheet terms in your own words: column, row, cell.
2. Identify three different types of data that can be entered into a spreadsheet cell.
3. Cells can be formatted to enhance the information. Name **one** way of doing this.
4. The data in a cell can be formatted to be displayed in a particular way. Name **two** different formatting options.
5. **(a)** Identify **two** different departments that would use a spreadsheet package.

   **(b)** Describe a task that could be carried out by each department.
6. Suggest **two** advantages of using a spreadsheet package.
7. Explain what is meant by the term **replication**.
8. Identify the function you would use to display the following:

   **(a)** the number of participants in a sports event

   **(b)** the participant with the fastest time in the 200m race

   **(c)** the total points for a participant taking part in the heptathlon

## Activity

Use a spreadsheet to help you calculate the cost of your Christmas wish list (or summer holiday packing list). You will need to carry out some research using the Internet.

Use the layout in this example of a Christmas wish list to help you.

| | A | B | C | D |
|---|---|---|---|---|
| 1 | Christmas Wish List | | | |
| 2 | | | | |
| 3 | **Item** | **Quantity** | **Price** | **Total** |
| 4 | | | | |
| 5 | | | | |
| 6 | | | | |
| 7 | | | | |
| 8 | **Overall Total** | | | |

## Key questions

1. You have just started working as an admin assistant in a local office. You have asked the owner to purchase spreadsheet software. Prepare a short report, using word processing software, to help persuade the owner to do this. Use the following headings in your report:
   - The purpose of a spreadsheet
   - Example of tasks that could be carried out using a spreadsheet package
   - The advantages of using a spreadsheet
2. A staff training day will be held in a local hotel. The following information is available.
   - Number of attendees: 12
   - Hire of room for one day: £195
   - Hire of all equipment: £120
   - Tea/coffee: £3.95 per person
   - Lunch: £19.95 per person
   - Name badges: £1.25 per person
   - Training manual: £4.75 per person
3. Complete the following spreadsheet, using appropriate formulae/functions. Format all cells appropriately.

| | A | B | C | D |
|---|---|---|---|---|
| 1 | EVENT EXPENDITURE | | | |
| 2 | | | | |
| 3 | Staff Training Day | | | |
| 4 | | | | |
| 5 | Item | Quantity | Unit Price | Total |
| 6 | Hire of Room | | | |
| 7 | Hire of Equipment | | | |
| 8 | Tea/Coffee | | | |
| 9 | Lunch | | | |
| 10 | Name Badges | | | |
| 11 | Training Manuals | | | |
| 12 | TOTAL | | | |
| 13 | | | | |
| 14 | Lunch as a percentage of the overall total | | | |
| 15 | | | | |

### Skill

- Literacy
- Numeracy
- Employability
- Skills for learning, life and work

## Summary

In this topic you have learned what is expected of you at both National 4 and National 5 levels, i.e. the skills you should be able to carry out at each level.

- You have learned what a spreadsheet package is, what it looks like and how it is used to help with mathematical calculations.
- You are able to describe what tasks are carried out using spreadsheet software by different departments in an organisation and the advantages of using this software.
- You have learned:
  - simple formulae: + – * /
  - complex functions: sum, average, maximum, minimum, count, IF, conditional formatting, linking cells within worksheets, using named cells, relative and absolute referencing
  - editing spreadsheets: sorting data, inserting/deleting columns/rows
  - creating fully-labelled charts/graphs from adjacent and non-adjacent cells
  - printing (extracts of) spreadsheets in a variety of formats: with/without gridlines, with/without row/column headings, landscape/portrait, value/formulae view.

## Learning Checklist

| | Skills, knowledge and understanding | Strength ☺ | 😐 | Weakness ☹ | Next steps |
|---|---|---|---|---|---|
| Formatting | I can align text in cell(s) | | | | • Refer to instructions<br>• Complete additional tasks<br>• Ask teacher for help |
| | I can add borders/shading to cell(s) | | | | • Refer to instructions<br>• Complete additional tasks<br>• Ask teacher for help |
| | I can format cells using different fonts, sizes, styles | | | | • Refer to instructions<br>• Complete additional tasks<br>• Ask teacher for help |
| | I can format cells to display currency, date, decimal places, percentage | | | | • Refer to instructions<br>• Complete additional tasks<br>• Ask teacher for help |

| | Skills, knowledge and understanding | Strength | | Weakness | Next steps |
|---|---|---|---|---|---|
| Formulae, functions and features | I can use basic arithmetic formulae to carry out calculations (+ – * /) | | | | • Refer to instructions<br>• Complete additional tasks<br>• Ask teacher for help |
| | I can use the sum function to carry out calculations | | | | • Refer to instructions<br>• Complete additional tasks<br>• Ask teacher for help |
| | I can use the average function to carry out calculations | | | | • Refer to instructions<br>• Complete additional tasks<br>• Ask teacher for help |
| | I can use the maximum function to carry out calculations | | | | • Refer to instructions<br>• Complete additional tasks<br>• Ask teacher for help |
| | "I can use the minimum function to carry out calculations" | | | | • Refer to instructions<br>• Complete additional tasks<br>• Ask teacher for help |
| | I can use the count function to carry out calculations | | | | • Refer to instructions<br>• Complete additional tasks<br>• Ask teacher for help |
| | I can use the IF function to carry out calculations with two possible answers | | | | • Refer to instructions<br>• Complete additional tasks<br>• Ask teacher for help |
| | I can use conditional formatting to display answers in different ways | | | | • Refer to instructions<br>• Complete additional tasks<br>• Ask teacher for help |
| | I can link cells within worksheets | | | | • Refer to instructions<br>• Complete additional tasks<br>• Ask teacher for help |
| | I can use named cells | | | | • Refer to instructions<br>• Complete additional tasks<br>• Ask teacher for help |
| | I can use relative and absolute cell references | | | | • Refer to instructions<br>• Complete additional tasks<br>• Ask teacher for help |
| Editing a spreadsheet | I can input data | | | | • Refer to instructions<br>• Complete additional tasks<br>• Ask teacher for help |
| | I can edit data | | | | • Refer to instructions<br>• Complete additional tasks<br>• Ask teacher for help |
| | I can sort data | | | | • Refer to instructions<br>• Complete additional tasks<br>• Ask teacher for help |
| | I can insert columns/rows | | | | • Refer to instructions<br>• Complete additional tasks<br>• Ask teacher for help |
| | I can delete columns/rows | | | | • Refer to instructions<br>• Complete additional tasks<br>• Ask teacher for help |

*(continued)*

| | Skills, knowledge and understanding | Strength | | Weakness | Next steps |
|---|---|---|---|---|---|
| Creating a simple chart from a specified range | I can create a pie chart | | | | • Refer to instructions<br>• Complete additional tasks<br>• Ask teacher for help |
| | I can create a bar/column chart | | | | • Refer to instructions<br>• Complete additional tasks<br>• Ask teacher for help |
| | I can create a line graph | | | | • Refer to instructions<br>• Complete additional tasks<br>• Ask teacher for help |
| | I can create a fully labelled chart/graph | | | | • Refer to instructions<br>• Complete additional tasks<br>• Ask teacher for help |
| | I can print a chart/graph as part of a worksheet | | | | • Refer to instructions<br>• Complete additional tasks<br>• Ask teacher for help |
| | I can print a chart/graph separately | | | | • Refer to instructions<br>• Complete additional tasks<br>• Ask teacher for help |
| Creating a chart from adjacent and non-adjacent cells | I can create a pie chart | | | | • Refer to instructions<br>• Complete additional tasks<br>• Ask teacher for help |
| | I can create a bar/column chart | | | | • Refer to instructions<br>• Complete additional tasks<br>• Ask teacher for help |
| | I can create a line graph | | | | • Refer to instructions<br>• Complete additional tasks<br>• Ask teacher for help |
| | I can create a fully labelled chart/graph | | | | • Refer to instructions<br>• Complete additional tasks<br>• Ask teacher for help |
| | I can print a chart/graph as part of a worksheet | | | | • Refer to instructions<br>• Complete additional tasks<br>• Ask teacher for help |
| | I can print a chart/graph separately | | | | • Refer to instructions<br>• Complete additional tasks<br>• Ask teacher for help |

| | Skills, knowledge and understanding | Strength ☺ | 😐 | Weakness ☹ | Next steps |
|---|---|---|---|---|---|
| Printing worksheets | I can print a worksheet showing values | | | | • Refer to instructions<br>• Complete additional tasks<br>• Ask teacher for help |
| | I can print a worksheet showing formulae | | | | • Refer to instructions<br>• Complete additional tasks<br>• Ask teacher for help |
| | I can print with/without gridlines | | | | • Refer to instructions<br>• Complete additional tasks<br>• Ask teacher for help |
| | I can print with/without row/ column headings | | | | • Refer to instructions<br>• Complete additional tasks<br>• Ask teacher for help |
| | I can print in portrait or landscape orientation | | | | • Refer to instructions<br>• Complete additional tasks<br>• Ask teacher for help |
| | I can print with headers/ footers | | | | • Refer to instructions<br>• Complete additional tasks<br>• Ask teacher for help |
| | I can print on one page | | | | • Refer to instructions<br>• Complete additional tasks<br>• Ask teacher for help |
| Printing extracts of worksheets | I can print a worksheet showing values | | | | • Refer to instructions<br>• Complete additional tasks<br>• Ask teacher for help |
| | I can print a worksheet showing formulae | | | | • Refer to instructions<br>• Complete additional tasks<br>• Ask teacher for help |
| | I can print with/without gridlines | | | | • Refer to instructions<br>• Complete additional tasks<br>• Ask teacher for help |
| | I can print with/without row/ column headings | | | | • Refer to instructions<br>• Complete additional tasks<br>• Ask teacher for help |
| | I can print in portrait or landscape orientation | | | | • Refer to instructions<br>• Complete additional tasks<br>• Ask teacher for help |
| | I can print with headers/ footers | | | | • Refer to instructions<br>• Complete additional tasks<br>• Ask teacher for help |
| | I can print on one page | | | | • Refer to instructions<br>• Complete additional tasks<br>• Ask teacher for help |

# 8 Databases

**You should already know**

- I can approach familiar and new situations with confidence when selecting and using appropriate software to solve increasingly complex problems or issues. **TCH 4-03a**
- I can use ICT effectively in different learning contexts across the curriculum to access, select and present relevant information in a range of tasks. **TCH 4-03b**
- To facilitate the transfer of skills between classroom and the world of work, I can select and use specialist equipment and appropriate software to develop administrative and management skills. **TCH 4-06a**
- Whilst working in a simulated or real workplace, I can select and use appropriate software to carry out a range of tasks which support business and entrepreneurial activities. **TCH 4-07a**

**In this chapter you will learn about:**

- The tasks you should be able to perform using a database package.
- The purpose of a database.
- The use of a database package by different departments in an organisation.
- The advantages of using a database.
- Editing a database.
- Altering the format of fields.
- Adding/deleting fields/records.
- Sorting information.
- Searching for information.
- Presenting information as a report.
- Printing information.

At National 4 level the databases used will be flat databases.

At National 5 level the databases used will be relational databases.

## What should I be able to do?

This part of the course requires you to solve business problems and present the solution using a database. The skills needed at both levels are shown below. National 5 pupils should be able to perform skills at both National 4 and National 5 levels.

## Quick-look list

If you want to quickly check what database tasks you should be able to perform, refer to the list shown below.

| Skill | Shown on page: |
|---|---|
| **Populating and editing a flat database and a relational database using forms**<br>• input and edit data making using of forms | <br>102 |
| • alter date format and decimal places<br>• add and delete field(s) and record(s) | 104<br>104 |
| **Manipulating information in a flat and a relational database**<br>• this will involve searching and sorting | <br>104 |
| **Searching the database using the following operators:**<br>• equals<br>• greater than<br>• less than | <br>105<br>105<br>106 |
| • greater than or equal to<br>• less than or equal to<br>• OR<br>• NOT | 105<br>105<br>106<br>106 |
| **Presenting information from a flat and a relational database in a report format, to a professional standard**<br>• produce a database report<br>• produce reports from a table or search | 106<br>106<br>106 |
| • produce reports from selected fields from a table or search | 106 |
| • insert a footer/header | 106 |
| **Print:**<br>• database<br>• search results<br>• forms<br>• reports<br>• to fit on one page | <br>107<br>107<br>107<br>107<br>107 |
| • specified fields | 107 |

## Databases

- A database is a collection of related information. A database allows us to search for information very quickly and to sort the information easily. The required data can be then be presented in the form of a printed report.

## Flat database

A **flat database** contains one file or table of data.

- each file is made up of a collection of records
- a record is the information about one person/thing (a collection of fields)
- a field is a single piece of information about the person/thing

For example, one record – for Melissa Hughes – contains seven fields.

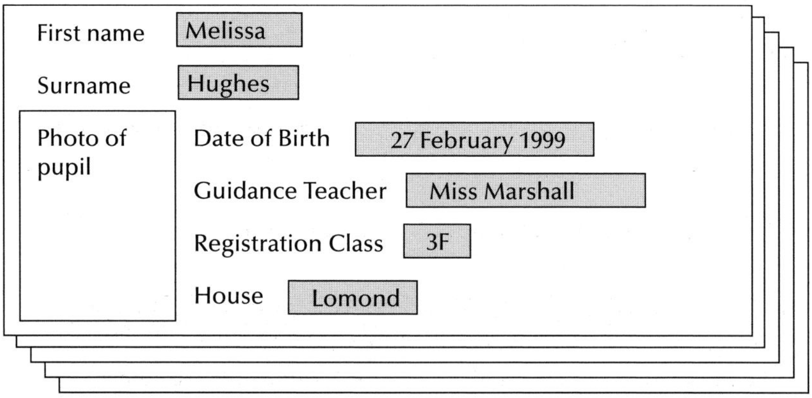

First name
Melissa
Surname
Hughes
Photo of pupil
Date of Birth
27 February 1999
Guidance Teacher
Miss Marshall
Registration Class
3F
House
Lomond


In the database file above, the information about the Guidance Teacher is not specific to the one pupil; several pupils will have the same Guidance Teacher. This means that the Guidance Teacher information will be repeated through the records. There are obviously disadvantages to having data repeated:

- It takes a long time to enter the data.
- It takes up more memory storage in the computer.
- If the data has to be edited, this would have to be carried out for every record.

## Relational database

A **relational database** can have more than one file or table of data. In the example shown, the same pupil record is displayed but the data is made up from two different tables. The two tables are linked through the Guidance Teacher Ref. No. field as this is shown in both tables. This will reduce the amount of data being repeated in the database. The Guidance Teacher Ref No. field is known as the **primary key**. Each Guidance Teacher would be allocated a unique number that would identify them. The name of the teacher cannot be a primary key as more than one teacher might have the same name.

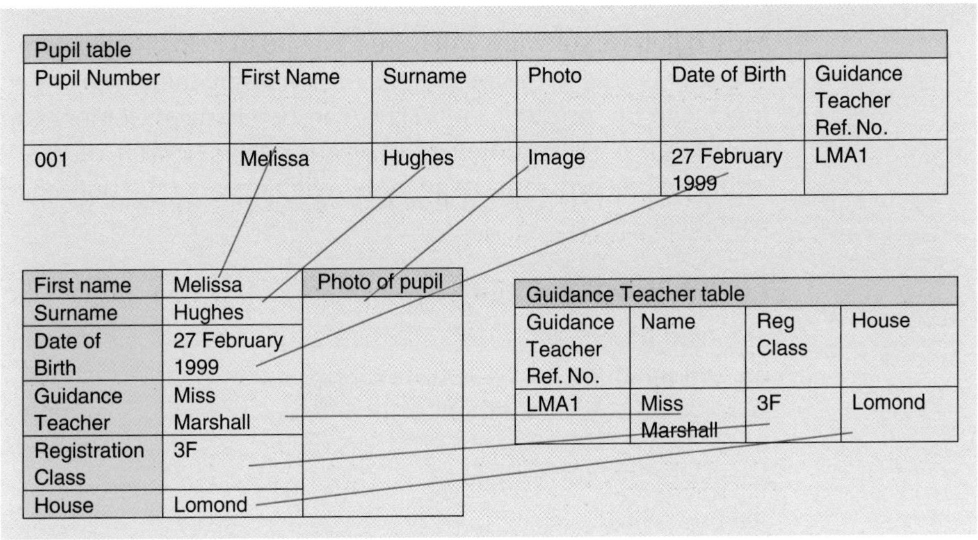

Pupil table
Pupil Number
First Name
Surname
Photo
Date of Birth
Guidance Teacher Ref. No.
001
Melissa
Hughes
Image
27 February 1999
LMA1
First name
Melissa
Surname
Hughes
Date of Birth
27 February 1999
Guidance Teacher
Miss Marshall
Registration Class
3F
House
Lomond
Photo of pupil
Guidance Teacher table
Guidance Teacher Ref. No.
Name
Reg Class
House
LMA1
Miss Marshall
3F
Lomond


You will learn more about functions of databases later in this chapter.

## Who uses databases in an organisation?

| Department | Use of databases |
|---|---|
| Human Resources/Personnel Department | • Store employee details |
| Sales Department | • Store customer details |
| Purchases Department | • Store supplier details |

An admin assistant working in any department may be regularly asked to update data on a database.

## Advantages of using databases

- Records can be found quickly using the **search** facility.
- Records can arranged into the required order quickly using the **sort** facility.
- A **query** can be used to create a **report.**
- The **mail merge** facility can be used to create personalised letters.

## Editing a database

An admin assistant would usually carry out tasks that involve populating and editing a database rather than creating a database.

## Populating a database

This means to **add data**. This can be done using forms or tables/ datasheets. Forms make it easier for the user to populate and edit data as only one record is displayed on screen at a time.

Most database software will have a wizard to help create a form. The user is able to customise the form by using the **design view**: logos can be inserted, fonts/sizes can be changed, footers can be added. A form footer will appear at the bottom of every individual record and a page footer will appear at the bottom of each page.

## Formatting

The field format describes the way the data is held. Fields can be formatted to display text, numbers, dates, currency or Yes/No. Dates can be formatted in different ways, for example 8 December 2012, 08/12/12 or 08Dec12. Numbers and currency can be formatted to show a specified number of decimal places.

## Adding/deleting fields/records

A database user can add fields or delete fields by using the design view in a table/datasheet or a form. A field can be added or inserted into an appropriate place in the design view. It must be formatted appropriately – text, number, etc. The user must return to the table/datasheet or form to fill in the appropriate details for all records. A field can be deleted from the design view. However, once a field has been deleted all the contents will automatically be deleted.

Whether working in table/datasheet or form view, a user can easily add new records. There will be an appropriate button for the user to click on to create a new blank record, and then the appropriate details must be keyed in. All new records will appear at the end of the database. A sort can be carried out to rearrange the records appropriately (see below). Any record can be selected and deleted (select the appropriate record, right click and choose delete), which will permanently remove it from the database, for example if an employee has left the organisation, their record must be deleted (under the Data Protection Act 1998, see Chapter 4, page 45).

## Sorting a database

Sorting data in a database can be carried out in different ways:

- **Alphabetical** – data can be sorted on a field (which has been formatted as text) to be shown in alphabetical order, for example by surname.
- **Numerical** – data can be sorted on a field (which has been formatted as number) to be shown in numerical order, for example by account number.
- **Chronological** – data can be sorted on a field (which has been formatted as date/time) to be shown in chronological (date/time) order, for example by date of birth.

Data can be sorted in any one of these ways into ascending or descending order.

A query can be created to carry out sorting tasks, which allows the results to be saved.

Sometimes it may be necessary to carry out a sort using more than one field. This is known as a **complex** sort. For example, if the data is to be organised into alphabetical order by surname, the database may contain more than one person with the same surname. It is possible to carry out a sort that will organise the surname field into alphabetical order first and then organise the first name field into alphabetical order next. For example:

| Surname | First Name |
|---|---|
| Smith | Alan |
| Smith | Grace |
| Smith | Henry |
| Smith | Sarah |
| Smith | Thomas |

## Searching a database

Searching for data in a database can be carried out in different ways. It is possible to search the database for an exact match in one or more fields or to use different operators as shown below:

| Operator | Explanation | Example(s) |
|---|---|---|
| = (equals) | Simply by keying in the word to be found **or** by keying in = before the word to be found. | • To find all employees working in the Sales Department: you would enter the word *Sales* in the *Department* field.<br>• To find all the customers who live in Glasgow with the surname Smith: you would enter the word *Glasgow* in the *Town* field and also enter the word *Smith* in the *Surname* field. |
| > (greater than) | Key in the greater than symbol (>) before a number/ date. | • To find all Sales Representatives who have sold goods for more than £10,000: you would enter >*10000* (the field should have been formatted as currency and therefore you do not enter the £ or ,) in the *Total Sales* field.<br>• To find all employees who were born after 31 December 1980: you would enter >*31/12/1980* in the *Date of Birth* field. |
| >= (greater than or equal to) | Key in the greater than symbol (>) followed by the equals symbol (=) before a number/ date. | • To find all Sales Representatives who have sold goods for £10,000 or more: you would enter >=*10000* (the field should have been formatted as currency and therefore you do not enter the £ or ,) in the *Total Sales* field.<br>• To find all employees who were born on or after 31 December 1980: you would enter >=*31/12/1980* in the *Date of Birth* field. |

| Operator | Explanation | Example(s) |
|---|---|---|
| < (less than) | Key in the less than symbol (<). | • To find all Sales Representatives who have sold goods for less than £10,000: you would enter *<10000* (the field should have been formatted as currency and therefore you do not enter the £ or ,) in the *Total Sales* field.<br>• To find all employees who were born before 31 December 1980: you would enter *<31/12/1980* in the *Date of Birth* field. |
| <= (less than or equal to) | Key in the less than symbol (<) followed by the equals symbol (=) before a number/ date. | • To find all Sales Representatives who have sold goods for £10,000 or less: you would enter *<=10000* (the field should have been formatted as currency and therefore you do not enter the £ or ,) in the *Total Sales* field.<br>• To find all employees who were born on or before 31 December 1980: you would enter*<=31/12/1980* in the *Date of Birth* field. |
| Or | Key in the first word to be found then the word OR followed by the second word to be found. | • To find all the customers who live in Glasgow or Edinburgh: you would enter *Glasgow OR Edinburgh* in the *Town* field.<br>• To find all the customers who live in Glasgow or Edinburgh with the surname Smith: you would enter *Glasgow OR Edinburgh* in the *Town* field **and** also enter the word *Smith* in the *Surname* field. |
| Not | Key in the word NOT followed by the word not to be included in the results. | • To find all the customers who do not live in Dumfries: you would enter *NOT Dumfries* in the *Town* field. |

**Watch point**

A query will allow searching and sorting to be carried out at the same time.

A query can be created to carry out searching tasks, which allows the results to be saved.

Searching for data in a database can be carried out on only one field, which is called a **simple** search; or on more than one field, which is called a **complex** search.

## Presenting information as a report

Reports are used to display data. They can be used to print out all the data in a database or to print selected fields/records generated from a query. Reports cannot be used for entering/ editing data – they are for displaying data.

- A report should always have an appropriate heading – this is usually entered in the report header and appears at the top of the report.
- A report footer can be used to display information at the end of the report.
- Page headers/footers can be inserted to display information (e.g. page numbers) at the top/bottom of each page.

Many software applications will allow the user to create a report using a wizard, which can do the following:

- Specify the table/query to be used
- Choose the layout for the report, for example in columns
- Specify the order of the fields, any groupings (to reduce the duplication of information)
- Change the page setup to landscape (to allow the report to fit on one page)
- Insert an appropriate heading

The database user can use the design view to carry out any additional editing/formatting to enhance the report, such as inserting graphics (company logos etc.) and formatting text (font, size, colour, etc.)

## Printing

When printing data from a database it is important that all the required information is visible. If it is not, then the user must go to the design view and adjust the appropriate field lengths so that the entries can be seen in full. Printing can be done as:

- table/datasheet
- query – showing the results of a search/sort, selected records/fields
- form – it is possible to print only one form
- report – effectively displaying the table/datasheet/query

Database software will allow the user to:

- create labels (which can be used for address labels or name badges)
- carry out a **mailmerge** (to produce personalised letters)

(See Chapter 9: Integrated software, page 116.)

**Watch point**

Always preview what is to be printed to check that everything is visible, fits on one page and that it looks professional.

**Activity**

The following database has been created to store the details of a local book club.

| Title | First Name | Surname | Street | Town/City | Postcode | DOB | Year joined |
|---|---|---|---|---|---|---|---|
| Miss | Anna | MacInnes | 28 Quality Street | Edinburgh | EH1 2WD | 25/07/1976 | 2004 |
| Mr | Liam | Smith | 13 Urquhart Place | Edinburgh | EH1 5TL | 17/12/1978 | 2003 |

*(continued)*

| Title | First Name | Surname | Street | Town/City | Postcode | DOB | Year joined |
|---|---|---|---|---|---|---|---|
| Mrs | Samantha | Marshall | 15 Mansion Gardens | Edinburgh | EH1 5TL | 01/01/1975 | 1995 |
| Mr | Sung | Lee | 33 Kelso Road | Dalkeith | EH13 4DJ | 11/06/1961 | 2001 |
| Mrs | Kirsty | Kerr | 63 Robinson Road | Dalkeith | EH13 4DJ | 24/08/1972 | 2001 |
| Mr | Kevin | Stewart | 86 Waterloo Street | Dalkeith | EH13 7NJ | 13/03/1967 | 2010 |
| Mr | John | Hailes | 28 Penilee Close | Dalkeith | EH14 9ZF | 15/09/1979 | 2010 |
| Mrs | Anne | Pollock | 8 Keith Avenue | Linlithgow | EH19 3CD | 27/04/1965 | 2011 |
| Mr | Ahmet | Mukherjee | 28 Jessfield Court | Edinburgh | EH2 4RS | 30/09/1972 | 2011 |
| Mr | Daniel | Scott | 48 Mount Pleasant | Musselburgh | EH23 7WS | 05/04/1980 | 2010 |
| Miss | Amelia | Ferguson | 18 Argyle Street | Roslin | EH24 5TQ | 31/01/1983 | 1989 |
| Mr | Derek | Ferguson | 18 Argyle Street | Roslin | EH24 5TQ | 03/10/1979 | 1993 |

Download the file *Database Example Task* from the Leckie & Leckie website (see page 5) and out the following instructions.

1. Create a form
2. Add the details for two new members:

| Title | First Name | Surname | Street | Town/City | Postcode | DOB | Year Joined |
|---|---|---|---|---|---|---|---|
| Mr | Brian | Yorke | 37 Clermiston Place | Edinburgh | EH1 4MS | 09/02/1987 | 2012 |
| Mrs | Bella | Marsh | 47 Warrington Avenue | Edinburgh | EH2 8WK | 31/03/1974 | 2012 |

3. Search for all members who became members of the book club before the year 2000.
4. Sort the results of this search into descending order of the year joined.
5. Produce a report of this information, showing all fields.
6. Insert a suitable report header and footer.
7. Print one copy of the report on one page.
8. Mr John Hailes has now left the book club. Delete his record.

9. Insert a new field for Telephone Number, formatted appropriately, and add the following information.

| Title | First Name | Surname | Telephone Number |
|---|---|---|---|
| Miss | Anna | MacInnes | 01316639832 |
| Mr | Liam | Smith | 01317739280 |
| Mrs | Samantha | Marshall | 01317382092 |
| Mr | Sung | Lee | 01318372813 |
| Mrs | Kirsty | Kerr | 01318364832 |
| Mr | Kevin | Stewart | 01318746382 |
| Mrs | Anne | Pollock | 01317262703 |
| Mr | Ahmet | Mukherjee | 01317362749 |
| Mr | Daniel | Scott | 01317261638 |
| Miss | Amelia | Ferguson | 01317568230 |
| Mr | Derek | Ferguson | 01317568230 |
| Mr | Brian | Yorke | 01317348329 |
| Mrs | Bella | Marsh | 01317463483 |

10. Format the date field to show the long date, i.e. 29 December 2012.
11. Search for all those members who were born on or after 1 January 1975.
12. Sort the database into alphabetical order of surname and first name.
13. Produce a report showing all members and their contact details.
14. Insert a suitable report header and footer.
15. Print one copy of the report on one page.

## ? Questions

1. Explain the following database terms in your own words: file, record, field.
2. Name the type of database that is made up of more than one table.
3. Explain:
   **(a)** What must be done to allow a new customer to be added to the database.
   **(b)** What must be done to remove fax numbers from the customer database.
4. Identify three different ways a field can be formatted.
5. **(a)** Identify two **different** departments that would use a database package.
   **(b)** Describe a task that may be carried out by each department.
6. Suggest **two** advantages of using a database package.

## Key questions

You have just started working as an admin assistant in the school office. You have asked the office manager to purchase database software.

1. Prepare a short presentation, using presentation software, to help persuade the office manager to do this. Use the following headings in your presentation:
   - The purpose of a database
   - Example of tasks that could be carried out using a database package
   - The advantages of using a database
2. You have decided to demonstrate the database package to the office manager. A small database containing pupil and guidance teacher information has been set up for this. Download the file *Database Key Question Task*. from the Leckie & Leckie website (see page 5) and carry out the following instructions:
   **(a)** The parents of Lynn Jones have telephoned the school and would like the name of her guidance teacher. Search the database for this information.
   **(b)** Ms Kay Watson would like you to tell her the names of the pupils in her year group. Search the database for this information.
   **(c)** Produce a database report that will show the pupils' names and dates of birth for each guidance teacher.
   **(d)** Insert an appropriate report header and footer.
   **(e)** Print this report on one page.

## Skill

- Literacy
- Numeracy
- Employability
- Skills for learning, life and work

## Activity

Download the file *Database Activity* from the Leckie & Leckie website (see page 5) and carry out the following instructions.

1. Create a form.
2. Complete the database for every pupil in your class.
3. Delete the sample record.
4. Sort the database into alphabetical order of surname and first name.
5. Produce a report showing all the fields.
6. Insert a suitable report header and footer.
7. Print the report on one page.

## Summary

In this topic you have learned what is expected of you at both National 4 and National 5 levels, i.e. the skills you should be able to carry out at each level.

- You have learned what a database package is, what it looks like and how it is used to help with storing, sorting and searching information.
- You are able to describe what tasks are carried out using database software by different departments in an organisation and the advantages of using this software.
- You have learned:
  - how to input/edit data using forms
  - how fields can be formatted, e.g. changing date format, decimal places
  - how fields/records can be added/deleted
  - how data can be sorted (alphabetical, numerical, chronological – ascending/descending): a simple sort on one field, or a complex sort on more than one field
  - how a database can be searched: a simple search on one field, or a complex search on more than one field
  - how to use a range of operators to find specific information, e.g. equals, greater than, greater than or equal to, less than, less than or equal to, OR, NOT
  - how to use reports to present information professionally (including the addition of headers/footers): from tables/searches/forms/selected fields
  - how to print with all fields visible (and to fit on one page): from database, search results, specified fields, forms, reports

## Learning Checklist

| | Skills, knowledge and understanding | Strength ☺ | 😐 | Weakness ☹ | Next steps |
|---|---|---|---|---|---|
| Populating/Editing | I can populate and edit a flat database using forms | | | | • Refer to instructions<br>• Complete additional tasks<br>• Ask teacher for help |
| | I can populate and edit a relational database using forms | | | | • Refer to instructions<br>• Complete additional tasks<br>• Ask teacher for help |
| | I can alter date format and decimal places | | | | • Refer to instructions<br>• Complete additional tasks<br>• Ask teacher for help |
| | I can add/delete field(s) and record(s) | | | | • Refer to instructions<br>• Complete additional tasks<br>• Ask teacher for help |

| | Skills, knowledge and understanding | Strength ☺ | 😐 | Weakness ☹ | Next steps |
|---|---|---|---|---|---|
| Manipulating Information – sorting and searching | I can sort a database on at least one field | | | | • Refer to instructions<br>• Complete additional tasks<br>• Ask teacher for help |
| | I can search a database using equals | | | | • Refer to instructions<br>• Complete additional tasks<br>• Ask teacher for help |
| | I can search a database using greater than | | | | • Refer to instructions<br>• Complete additional tasks<br>• Ask teacher for help |
| | I can search a database using greater than or equal to | | | | • Refer to instructions<br>• Complete additional tasks<br>• Ask teacher for help |
| | I can search a database using less than | | | | • Refer to instructions<br>• Complete additional tasks<br>• Ask teacher for help |
| | I can search a database using less than or equal to | | | | • Refer to instructions<br>• Complete additional tasks<br>• Ask teacher for help |
| | I can search a database using OR | | | | • Refer to instructions<br>• Complete additional tasks<br>• Ask teacher for help |
| | I can search a database using NOT | | | | • Refer to instructions<br>• Complete additional tasks<br>• Ask teacher for help |
| Presenting information in a report | I can produce a report from a database | | | | • Refer to instructions<br>• Complete additional tasks<br>• Ask teacher for help |
| | I can produce a report from a table or search | | | | • Refer to instructions<br>• Complete additional tasks<br>• Ask teacher for help |
| | I can insert a footer/header | | | | • Refer to instructions<br>• Complete additional tasks<br>• Ask teacher for help |
| | I can produce a report from selected fields from a table or search | | | | • Refer to instructions<br>• Complete additional tasks<br>• Ask teacher for help |

| | Skills, knowledge and understanding | Strength ☺ | 😐 | Weakness ☹ | Next steps |
|---|---|---|---|---|---|
| Printing | I can print a database with all fields visible | | | | • Refer to instructions<br>• Complete additional tasks<br>• Ask teacher for help |
| | I can print search results | | | | • Refer to instructions<br>• Complete additional tasks<br>• Ask teacher for help |
| | I can print forms | | | | • Refer to instructions<br>• Complete additional tasks<br>• Ask teacher for help |
| | I can print reports | | | | • Refer to instructions<br>• Complete additional tasks<br>• Ask teacher for help |
| | I can print to fit on one page | | | | • Refer to instructions<br>• Complete additional tasks<br>• Ask teacher for help |

# 3

# Communication in Administration

# 9 Integrated software packages

**You should already know**

- How to create documents using word processing software.
- How to create a database file and use the functions of database software.
- How to create a spreadsheet and use the functions of spreadsheet software.
- How to search and extract information using the Internet.

**In this chapter you will learn about:**

- What is meant by the term 'integrated software'.
- Advantages of using an integrated software package.
- How to integrate data from other IT applications into a business document to enhance it.
- How to integrate data from other IT applications dynamically into a business document to enhance it.

## What is an integrated software package?

An integrated software package combines several applications in the one computer program. These are typically: word processing, spreadsheet, database, presentation, graphics and communications. Commonly used integrated software packages include Microsoft Office and AppleWorks.

### Advantages of using an integrated software package

- On-screen layouts and instructions are similar across the package – this makes it easier to learn and use all applications. Take a look at the ribbon below from a Microsoft Word document and compare it to Microsoft spreadsheet, database and presentation documents – they are all similar. This makes it easier to learn how to use each of the applications in the one integrated software package.

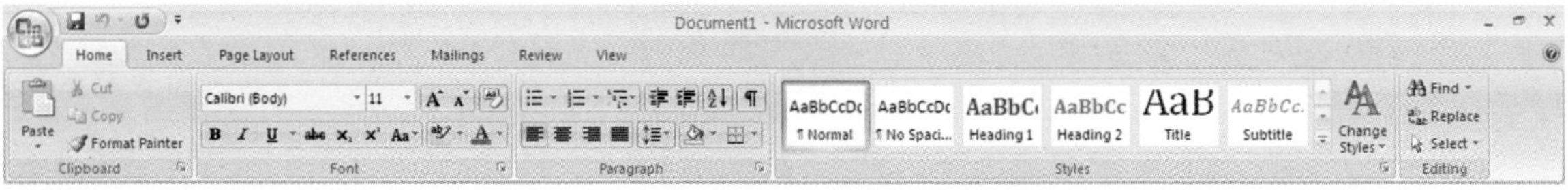

- Data is easily transferred between packages; for example, a chart created on a spreadsheet can easily be copied and pasted into a word processing document.
- An integrated software package can be cheaper than buying software packages individually.
- Mailmerge – information contained in a database file can be merged with a word processing document to personalise the document (address labels, name badges, letters, etc.)
- Dynamic linkage – changes made to data in one application can be automatically updated in another application.

**Watch point**

When merging a database with another document ensure that all the appropriate fields are present and in the correct location.

## Activity

**1.** Download the file *Health and Safety Memo* from the Leckie & Leckie website (see page 5).

**(a)** Action and delete the comments within the file.
**(b)** Save as *Updated Health and Safety Memo.*
**(c)** Print one copy of the amended memo.

**2. (a)** Download the file *Sales Memo* from the Leckie & Leckie website (see page 5).

**(i)** Action and delete the comments within the file.
**(ii)** Save the file as *Sales Memo July*.

**(b)** Download the file *Target v Actual Sales July* from the Leckie & Leckie website (see page 5) and make the following changes.

**(i)** Change the month from July to August
**(ii)** Update the Target and Actual Sales as follows:

| | Target | Actual |
|---|---|---|
| Tom Hunt | 550 | 600 |
| Patricia Griffiths | 250 | 350 |
| Mhari Hogan | 250 | 400 |

**(iii)** Ensure the *Sales Memo July* has been updated.
**(iv)** Save the *Sales Memo July* as *Sales Memo August*.
**(v)** Print one copy of the amended memo.

**3.** Download the file *Training Letter* from the Leckie & Leckie website (see page 5).

**(a)** Action and delete comments within the file.
**(b)** Save as *Updated Training letter*.
**(c)** Print one copy of the file.

*(continued)*

**4. (a)** Download the file *Leisure Letter* from the Leckie & Leckie website (see page 5).

- **(i)** Action and delete comments within the file.
- **(ii)** Save the letter as *Leisure Letter 1*.
- **(iii)** Print one copy of the letter.

**(b)** Download the file *Leisure Classes* from the Leckie & Leckie website (see page 5)

- **(i)** Delete the Body Pump class taking place on Friday at 4 pm.
- **(ii)** Change the time of the Kettle bells class on a Thursday to 7 pm.
- **(iii)** Insert a new record – Junior Gym – which will take place on a Tuesday at 4 pm. It lasts for 30 minutes and the maximum class size is 10.
- **(iv)** Ensure the file *Leisure Letter* has been updated.
- **(v)** Save *Leisure Letter* as *Leisure Letter 2*.
- **(vi)** Print one copy of the amended letter.

## Skill

- Decision-making
- ICT
- Literacy
- Employability
- Skills for learning, life and work

## Key questions

**1.** Download the file *Event Info* from the Leckie & Leckie website (see page 5).

- **(a)** Action and delete comments within the file.
- **(b)** Save as *Event Info sheet 1*.
- **(c)** Print one copy of the amended document.

**2. (a)** Download the file *Berlin Trip* from the Leckie & Leckie website (see page 5).

- **(i)** Action and delete comments within the file.
- **(ii)** Save as *Berlin Trip 1*.
- **(iii)** Print one copy of the amended document.

**(b)** Mr and Mrs Jones wish to fly from Edinburgh to Berlin on the first Monday of next month and return on the first Friday of next month. Use the Internet to find out the price of a return flight.

- **(i)** Update the spreadsheet *Costings for Mr and Mrs Jones* using the information you obtained from the Internet.
- **(ii)** Ensure letter *Berlin Trip* has been updated.
- **(iii)** Save the letter as *Berlin Trip 2*.
- **(iv)** Print one copy of the amended document.

## GO! Activity

**1.** Download the file *Conference Delegates* from the Leckie & Leckie website (see page 5).

- **(a)** Create name badges for the delegates.
- **(b)** Save the file as *Name Badges*.
- **(c)** Print one copy of the document.

**2.** **(a)** Download the file *Customer Database* from the Leckie & Leckie website (see page 5).

- **(i)** Create address labels for letters to be sent to the customers.
- **(ii)** Saves the file as Address labels.
- **(iii)** Print one copy of the address labels.

**(b)** The following changes should be made to the file *Customer Database*.

- **(i)** James Marley has moved to 765 Perth Road, Pitlochry, PH16 2XC – update his details.
- **(ii)** Poppy Smith is no longer a customer – delete her record.
- **(iii)** Add another record to the database – Mrs Gail Dolan, 324 Ferniegair Road, Hamilton, ML3 4FL.
- **(iv)** Ensure the address labels have been updated.
- **(v)** Save the address labels as *Address labels 1*.
- **(vi)** Print one copy of the amended address labels.

## Summary

An integrated software package combines several applications in the one computer program. There are many advantages of using integrated software packages, such as: on-screen layouts are similar; data can be transferred between packages; mail merge is available and dynamic linkage is possible. It can also be cheaper to buy an integrated software package than buying software packages individually.

## Learning Checklist

| Skills, knowledge and understanding | Strength | | Weakness | Next steps |
|---|---|---|---|---|
| **1.** I understand what is meant by the term **integrated software**. | | | | |
| **2.** I understand the advantages of using an integrated software package. | | | | |
| **3.** I can integrate data from other IT applications into a business document to enhance it. | | | | |
| **4.** I can integrate data from other IT applications dynamically into a business document to enhance it. | | | | |

# 10 Use technology to extract information and evaluate sources of information

**You should already know**

- Throughout all my learning, I can use search facilities of electronic sources to access and retrieve information, recognising the importance this has in my place of learning, at home and in the workplace. **TCH 2-01b**

**In this chapter you will learn about:**

- Uses of the Internet.
- Terms associated with using the Internet to extract information.
- Advantages of using the Internet as a source of information.
- How to determine whether an Internet website is reliable.
- The consequences of using unreliable Internet sources of information.
- Uses of an intranet.
- Advantages of using an intranet.

## The Internet

The **Internet** is a network of connected computers (computers linked together over a large geographical area – across the world). It is Wide Area Network (**WAN**).

The Internet has many uses for an organisation:

- Researching:
  - travel/accommodation information – availability, costs, etc.
  - latest foreign travel advice
  - travel routes (for example, for salespeople)
  - latest travel information (accidents, traffic jams on routes, flight delays etc.)
  - competitors' prices/promotions
  - potential supplier's deals
  - latest news
  - government publications
- Advertising the organisation's products and job vacancies.
- E-commerce (electronic commerce):
  - selling products online – this allows access to a global market, 24/7, which could increase the organisation's sales and profits
  - buying products from suppliers: prices, delivery dates and other factors can be compared before selecting the best deal
- Booking travel/hotel accommodation
- Using e-mail to contact customers, suppliers etc.
- Web conferencing: for face-to-face discussions by users in different locations
- Gaining customer feedback and reviews

## Searching for and extracting/downloading relevant information

A **web browser** is a software application used to access, retrieve and view information on the Internet.

To access information on the Internet, a website address (also known as a Uniform Resource Locator – **URL**) can be keyed in, or, if the user is unsure of the website address then keywords can be typed into a **search engine.**

A search engine makes it possible to find a specific item of information from the vast amount of data stored on the web. To use a search engine you type in the words that describe the information you are interested in and a (usually) long list of pages that contain related content will appear. Examples of search engines include Google, Yahoo!, Bing and Ask.

Once you either key in the website address or choose from the list displayed by the search engine, the **homepage** of the website is usually displayed. The homepage is the first page you see on a website and will often have general information about the company, its history, products and contents of the website. The home page will usually contain a **search box** – this allows the user to type in keywords to find relevant information contained *within* the website.

Most websites contain **hyperlinks**, which allow the user to go from one part of the website to another. When you move your mouse over the hyperlink it usually changes from an arrow to a hand and the link becomes underlined.

Information from a website can be **downloaded** onto an individual's computer. Usually it is better to copy the text required and paste it to a word/presentation document (omitting adverts, pictures etc) before printing.

**Bookmarks/Favourites** allow the user to store the addresses of frequently visited websites. This avoids wasting time either keying in the website address in full each time, or using a search engine.

## Advantages of using the Internet as a source of information

- Information is usually up-to-date – many websites are updated on a regular basis to give the latest prices, availability etc.
- A vast range of information is available – this gives users access to much more information than they previously could have gathered.
- Websites may give more detailed information than printed material like brochures or catalogues – many hotels have 'virtual tours' on their website.
- Convenience – users can access information at a time when it is convenient to them.
- Information is instantly available, for example the seat availability is shown when booking flights.

## Accessing reliable information on the Internet

- Users of the Internet must be selective about the sources they take information from. Anyone can create a website with information that may be inaccurate and therefore unreliable.
- Users relying on the Internet for accurate information should only use websites that are reputable or from a well-known organisation, for example government websites or major news websites.

- Users should also try to ensure they use a website that is updated on a regular basis. These websites are more likely to be accurate.
- Users should look carefully at the website – if the site looks poorly designed and substandard it probably has not been created by a professional and chances are that it will not be reliable.
- Use a secure website, particularly if using credit card or other method of payment over the Internet. A secure website will have a padlock sign on it or **https** in the address, showing that it is a verified website and uses encryption (see Chapter 4, page 45).

> **Watch point**
> You should be able to evaluate the source of information used – is it reliable, up-to-date and secure?

> **Watch point**
> Check the hyperlinks – reputable companies often link to one another. See which sites the website you are on links to. Then go on Google and search it to ensure it exists.

## Consequences of using unreliable Internet sources of information

Using out-of-date information could have a damaging effect on a business, for example using an out-of-date train timetable could result in staff missing important meetings and thus losing orders/sales. Using out-of-date information is worse than having no information at all!

As anyone can post information on a website it is important to check that it is accurate and free from bias (this is when someone puts their opinion/slant on the information and does not stick to fact). This could influence your results, for example if you are writing a report you may include inaccuracies and bias that does not lead to your desired outcome.

If secure websites are not used and websites are hacked, sensitive/personal information may be stolen. This could include credit card and bank details! This could result in someone using your information to gain access to your bank account.

For the purpose of this course you should be able to:

- use a search engine to find relevant websites
- use a search box within a website to find relevant information
- use hyperlinks to take you from one website/webpage to another
- extract relevant information from webpages
- download relevant information to your computer

## Intranet

An **intranet** is an internal network used to share information *within* an organisation.

Employees of the organisation can access information on company events, current policies (such as health and safety), staff newsletters, product information and price lists, internal telephone numbers etc. The intranet may also store files that employees need to download and complete, such as expense claim forms, accident reports etc.

The intranet can also be used for internal e-mail, electronic diary facilities and sharing software within an organisation.

### Advantages of an intranet

- All employees have access to the same current information.
- Time is saved as information needs only to be updated once.
- Cost savings – all information is stored electronically, reducing paper and photocopying costs.
- Communication (particularly in large organisations) is improved through use of systems such as internal e-mail and electronic diaries.

For the purpose of this unit you should be able to:

- access an intranet
- search an intranet
- extract relevant information from an intranet

### Make the link

- In subjects like English, Modern Studies and Geography you could use the Internet to research current information (news reports etc.).
- In History you could use the Internet to research historical events.
- In a variety of subjects you could use revision websites to enhance your knowledge of the subject.
- In the Administration and IT Added Value Unit (National 4) and Assignment (National 5) you will be required to access the Internet to source reliable information.

### Activity

Go to www.bbc.co.uk/webwise and select the links for *Using the Web, About the Internet* and *Internet Basics*.

1. Work your way through each of the lessons:
   **(a)** What is the Internet?
   **(b)** Staying safe online.
2. For additional practice you could select *Searching – searching the Internet* and *Internet search challenge*.

## ? Questions

1. Give **three** examples of when an organisation may use the Internet for research purposes.
2. Define the following terms associated with the Internet:
   **(a)** Web browser
   **(b)** Search engine
   **(c)** Search box
   **(d)** Hyperlink
   **(e)** Download
   **(f)** Bookmarks/Favourites
3. List **three** advantages of using the Internet as a source of information.
4. State why it is important to be selective about which Internet sources are used for information.
5. Explain how you know if an Internet website is reliable.
6. Give **three** consequences of using unreliable Internet sources of information.
7. Describe an intranet.
8. State **three** uses and advantages of an intranet.

## ★ Key questions

Complete the following exercise.

To: pupil@school.sch.uk

From: Dylansmith@yha.com

Date: Today's

Subject: SALES CONFERENCE IN DUBLIN

I wish to travel to Paris on the first Monday of next month and return on Wednesday (of the same week). I would prefer to fly from Glasgow. This means that I need to travel from Inverness (by either bus or train) the day before.

I will require accommodation in Glasgow for Sunday and Wednesday nights, and also for the nights I am in Paris. I would prefer to stay in 4 or 5 star hotels.

Use the Internet to research the required information (travel times, hotel names and addresses). **E-mail the relevant information to me** (you should have a note of my e-mail address).

Please do not book, as I wish to check it over and then confirm the flights and accommodation arrangements before booking.

### Skill

- Decision-making
- ICT
- Literacy
- Employability
- Skills for learning, life and work

## Activity

***Individually or in pairs***

1. Use a search engine to access a number of different websites. Complete the following checklist to help you evaluate whether each website would be a reliable source of information.

| Name of website | | | |
|---|---|---|---|
| Is it from a reputable or well-known organisation? | | | |
| Check the date – check to see if there is a 'last updated' date on the page or site. | | | |
| Look at the site's design – is it poorly designed/amateurish? | | | |
| Check the links | | | |
| Evaluation – do you think this website is a reliable source of information | | | |

2. You are an admin assistant in your local high school. You have been given the task of organising the S5/6 prom. Read the following e-mail from the organising committee and find the information required.

To: Administrative assistant

From: Kirstin Dolan, School Captain

Subject: Our Prom!!!

We are all so excited about the prom on 14 June.

We are unsure about a venue – can you find information on **two** venue/hotels that would be willing to host a prom? I think there will be approximately 100 people attending. We are happy to travel approximately 5 miles from school.

Can you find out the names of **two** local bus companies?

Lastly, we would love a ceilidh band to play at the prom. Can you find the names of **two** ceilidh bands? I think they would be able to travel a distance to play at the prom.

If you print out the information we require (perhaps the homepages of each website visited) it would help us to make decisions about the above.

Thanks
Kirstin

## Activity

*Group or whole class*

**Graffiti board**

Resources required:

- Eight sheets of A3 paper
- Marker pens

On pieces of A3 paper the teacher should write the following headings:

- Advantages of using the Internet as a source of information
- Disadvantages of using the Internet as a source of information
- Reliability of websites
- Information found on the Internet

The class should be divided into four groups, each with a headed sheet of A3 paper. Give the groups 2 minutes to 'grafitti' their thoughts on their A3 sheet. After 2 minutes the groups should move to the next sheet of A3 paper and 'grafitti' their thoughts on that particular question. This should continue until the groups have been around all the A3 sheets of paper. This should be completed in silence.

Once the group returns to their original piece of A3 paper they should discuss what others have written. They should then create an information sheet with what they consider relevant answers.

Groups should be prepared to share their work with the rest of the class.

## Summary

The Internet has many uses for an organisation. It is a very valuable source of information and there are many advantages of using the Internet:

- Information is usually up-to-date.
- A vast range of information is available.
- Websites may give more detailed information.
- It is easily accessed and information is instantly available.

Terms associated with the Internet include:

- web browser
- search engine

*(continued)*

- home page
- hyperlinks
- download
- bookmark/favourites

When using the Internet as a source of information it is important that only reliable websites are used. Using out-of-date information or biased information could have consequences for the business and may not lead to the desired outcome the business would hope for. If secure websites are not used then personal information may be stolen. The user should check that the website is:

- from a reputable source or a well-known organisation
- updated on a regular basis
- well-designed
- secure

An intranet is an internal network used to share information within an organisation, for example events, current policies, staff newsletters, etc. Downloadable forms like expense claim forms or accident reports may also be stored on the intranet to allow employees to access and complete them. Internal e-mail, electronic diary facilities and sharing software are also features of an intranet.

The advantages of using the intranet include:

- All employees have access to the same current information.
- Information needs only to be updated once.
- As information is stored electronically, paper and photocopying costs are reduced.
- Communication is improved through use of internal e-mail, electronic diaries etc.

## Learning Checklist

| | Skills, knowledge and understanding | Strength ☺ | 😐 | Weakness ☹ | Next steps |
|---|---|---|---|---|---|
| Populating/Editing | **1.** I understand uses of the Internet | | | | |
| | **2.** I understand terms associated with using the Internet to extract information | | | | |
| | **3.** I understand advantages of using the Internet as a source of information | | | | |
| | **4.** I understand how to determine whether an Internet website is reliable | | | | |
| | **5.** I understand the consequences of using unreliable Internet source of information | | | | |
| | **6.** I understand uses of the intranet | | | | |
| | **7.** I understand advantages of using an intranet | | | | |

# 11 Multimedia and presentations

**You should already know**

- I can approach familiar and new situations with confidence when selecting and using appropriate software to solve increasingly complex problems or issues. **TCH 4-03a**
- I can use ICT effectively in different learning contexts across the curriculum to access, select and present relevant information in a range of tasks. **TCH 4-03b**

**In this chapter you will learn about:**

- The use of multimedia and presentation software.
- The advantages of using presentation software.
- The functions of presentation software used to prepare and communicate simple information.

**Make the Link**

You may be asked to produce a presentation in other subjects. Remember that using presentation software will allow you to present information - including graphics, movies and sounds - in way that is more interesting for your audience. Projects in any subject can be enhanced through the use of presentation software.

## Use of multimedia and presentation software

Presentations are used to pass information to an audience. For example, a Training Officer may deliver induction training to new employees and a Sales Manager may deliver a presentation on the sales targets to Sales Representatives. It is essential that the presenter creates a good impression, and that the presentation is readable, interesting and easy to understand. A variety of equipment/software can be used to prepare and present information.

### Software

- **Presentation software** – used to prepare slides that can contain text, graphics, sound, animation. This can be set up to be shown automatically to the audience or the pace can be controlled by only moving on to the next slide when appropriate, allowing for discussion to take place. This software would be used with a multimedia/data projector.
- **Word processing/DTP software** – used to prepare handouts to accompany a presentation, which can be referred to at a later date. Text and graphics can be included.
- **Spreadsheet software** – used to prepare graphs/charts that can be included in a handout or displayed on screen when connected to a multimedia/data projector.

## Equipment

- **Multimedia/data projector** – allows images on the computer to be displayed on a large screen. Any file created on the computer can be seen by the audience, for example charts/graphs created using spreadsheet software.
- **Interactive whiteboard** – this allows data to be displayed to the audience, which can be edited/changed during the presentation.

## Advantages of using presentation software

- Information can be formatted to emphasise important information.
- Presentation can be delivered at a pace to suit the audience, allowing for discussion to take place.
- Slides can be created/edited very quickly for a different audience.
- Information from other applications can also be included in the presentation (graphs/charts created in a spreadsheet package).
- Printed handouts can accompany a presentation (so audience can refer back to in their own time).

## Quick-look list

If you want to quickly check what functions you should be able to perform using presentation software, refer to the list shown below.

| Skill | Shown on page: |
|---|---|
| • Insert, edit and format text | 132 |
| • Align text | 132 |
| • Insert graphics | 132 |
| • Use bullets | 132 |
| • Create chart(s) and/or table(s) | 132 |
| • Add and delete a slide | 133 |
| • Animate text/objects | 134 |
| • Import date from other applications/Internet | 134 |
| • Change slide content layout | 134 |
| • Apply slide transitions | 134 |
| • Change slide order | 134 |
| • Apply and change background and colour scheme | 135 |
| • Insert footer objects | 135 |
| • Insert action buttons | 135 |
| • Use slide master | 135 |
| • Print presentation in slide and handout format | 136 |

## Functions of presentation software

Many of the skills learned in word processing can also be used when working with presentation software.

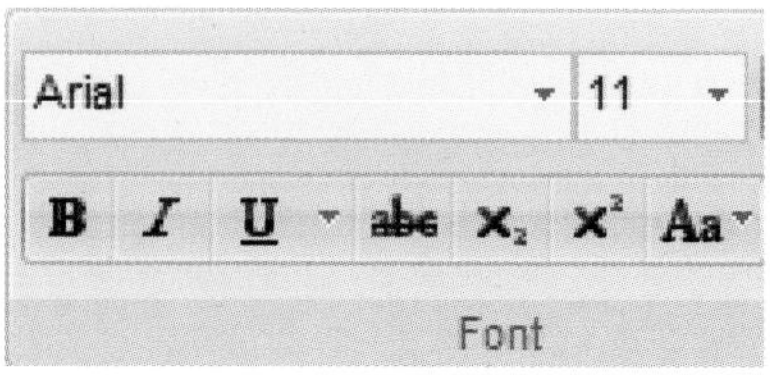


### *Insert, edit and format text*

Text can be inserted and easily edited. Text can be formatted using different fonts, sizes and styles.

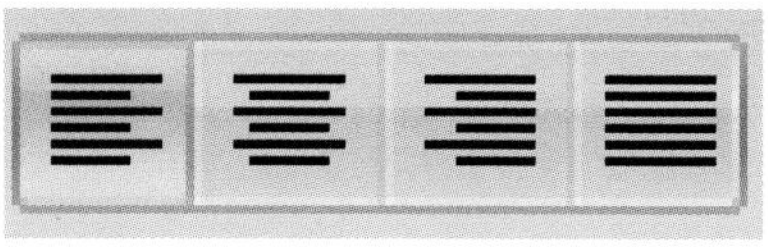

### *Align text*

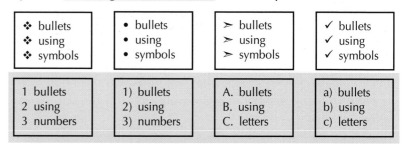

Text on the slide can be aligned – left aligned, centred, right-aligned or fully justified.

### *Insert graphics*

Graphics can be inserted – this can be done using Clipart or from a picture that has been scanned, downloaded from the Internet or uploaded from a digital camera. Graphics help to make the presentation more interesting for the audience.

### *Use bullets or numbers*

Bulleted lists are useful when presenting information, and presentation software allows the user to reveal one line of bulleted text at a time. Bullets can be shown using a variety of symbols or using numbers/letters. For example:

| | | | |
|---|---|---|---|
| ❖ bullets<br>❖ using<br>❖ symbols | • bullets<br>• using<br>• symbols | ➢ bullets<br>➢ using<br>➢ symbols | ✓ bullets<br>✓ using<br>✓ symbols |
| 1 bullets<br>2 using<br>3 numbers | 1) bullets<br>2) using<br>3) numbers | A. bullets<br>B. using<br>C. letters | a) bullets<br>b) using<br>c) letters |

### *Create chart(s) and/or table(s)*

Charts and tables can be included in the presentation. Most presentation software will allow the chart or table to be created in the presentation rather than in another program.

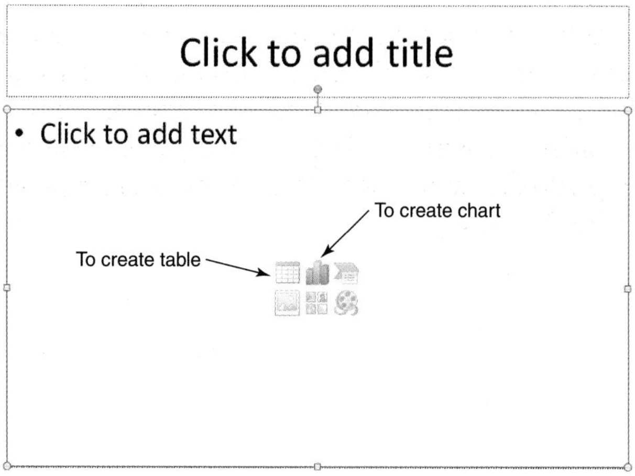

However, it is also possible, using integrated software, to copy and paste a chart or table made in another software package, for example a spreadsheet or word processed document. (see page 116.)

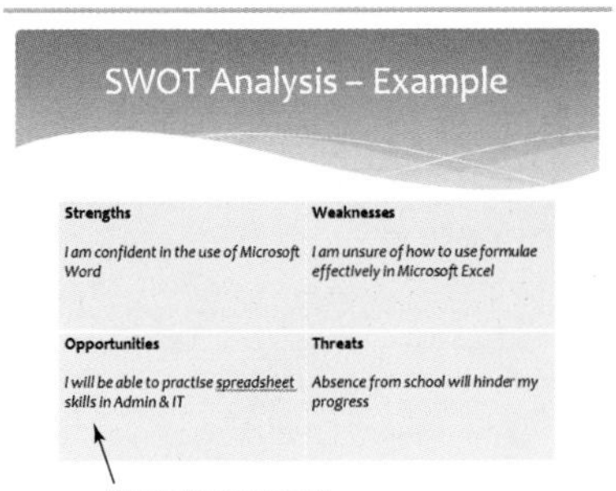


Copied from a word processing document

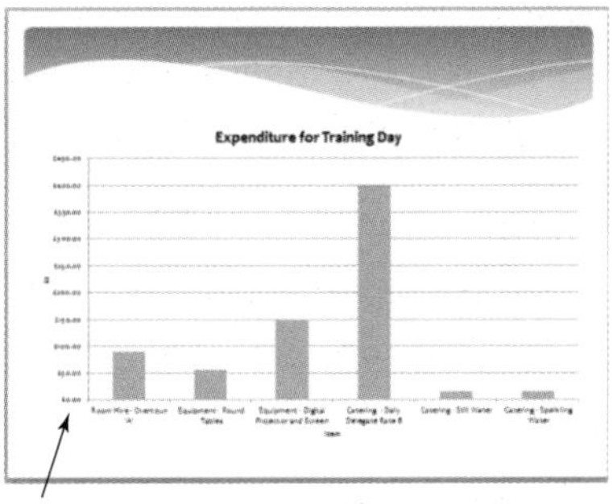


Copied from a spread sheet

### *Slide order*

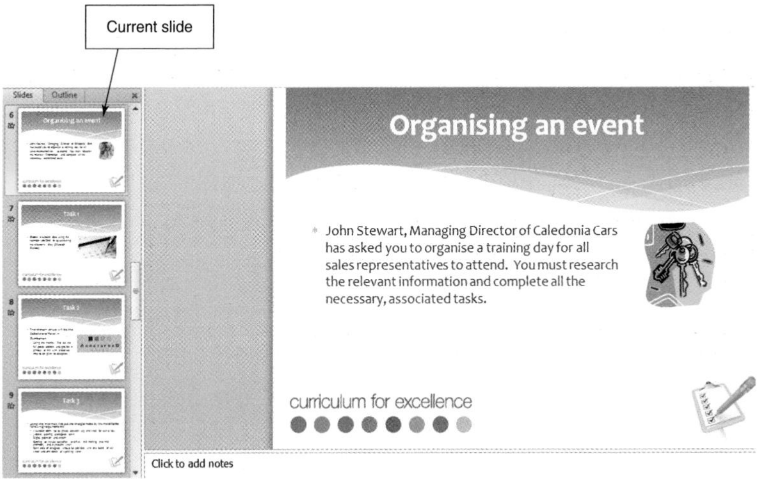


When a slideshow presentation is being prepared it is usual for the current slide to be shown to the right-hand side of the screen and the order of the slides to be shown in a smaller format to the left. Every time a new slide is added/created it will appear at the end of the presentation to become the next slide. If you want to change the order it is possible to use a function (in Microsoft PowerPoint this is called 'Slide Sorter') to allow you to sort the slides into any order you wish. To delete a slide you can simply select the appropriate slide and choose delete from the appropriate menu or press the Delete key.

> **Watch point**
> Do not use too many different animations for the one slide as this can be distracting for the audience.

*Animating text/objects*

One of the advantages of using presentation software is the use of **animation** to make a presentation more interesting for the audience. This allows the user to set the text/objects to appear on screen at the click of the mouse button/keyboard key. Text and objects can appear on screen in a variety of different ways, for example they can be set to fly in (from the bottom, left, etc.) or fade in. It is also possible to animate text/objects for emphasis and to exit the slide. Examples of animation:

*Importing data from other applications/Internet*

Like any other package it is possible to use the copy and paste function to copy text/objects from another package into a presentation. Likewise, it is possible to find appropriate text and objects from the Internet and to copy these into the presentation.

*Change slide content layout*

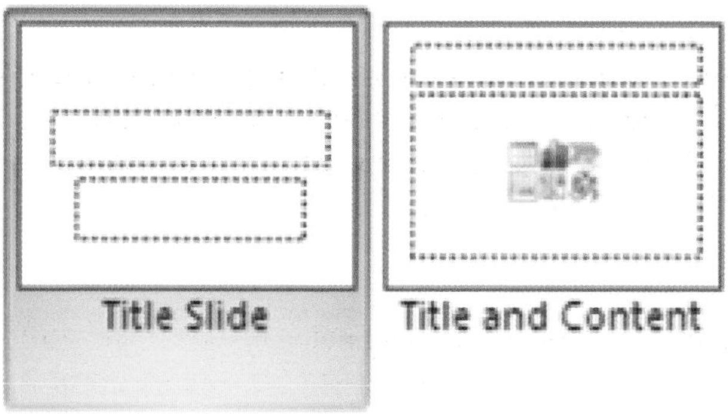


A presentation will usually start with a title slide, showing an appropriate title (and subtitle). There is a range of different slide layouts that can be used to vary the slides to suit the information. The example shown above would allow the user to insert a title for the slide and then insert text (usually in the form of a bulleted list), graphics (from Clipart or file), chart or table.

> **Watch point**
> Choose **one** slide transition style – too many variations will not improve the presentation!

*Apply slide transitions*

A slide transition can be set up to allow the change from one slide to the next to be more interesting for the audience. For example, the first slide may fade away and the next slide will be revealed slowly or quickly.

### *Apply and change background, colour scheme and/or apply design templates*

Slides in the presentation (all or selected) can be given a background colour or a colour scheme, often to match the content of the presentation. For example, if you were asked to create a presentation about your school you could choose a background colour or a colour scheme that reflects the colour of your school tie. The background colour of each slide could match with the main colour in the tie and the titles and text content could match with a different colour.

It is also possible to create your own background using a picture or photograph.

Presentation software usually comes with design templates that allow a user to choose a design rather than create one. It is possible to edit the colours of the design to personalise it. Examples of design templates:

### *Insert footer objects*

Footers can be added to a presentation in the same way that they can be added to a word processed document. Footers can be used to display dates, slide numbers or an appropriate graphic, such as a company logo.

### *Insert action buttons*

Action buttons are built-in shapes that can be added to the presentation to make an action occur when the mouse is clicked or moved over the button. Actions include move to the next slide, move to the previous slide, return the first slide; and the buttons are designed to look like the action they carry out.

### *Slide master*

Master slides are used to set the layout and standard formatting on **all** slides in the presentation. The placeholders (for example the title box), the objects and the formatting (font size, style etc.) on the master slides are automatically applied to every slide in the presentation.

The title slide master will contain the placeholders for the presentation title (and subtitle).

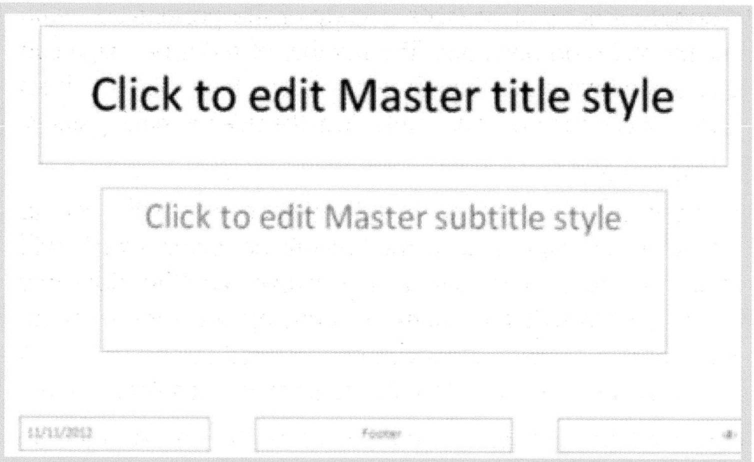

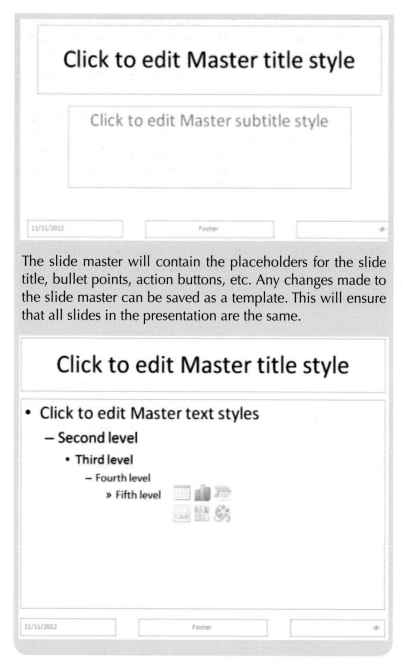

The slide master will contain the placeholders for the slide title, bullet points, action buttons, etc. Any changes made to the slide master can be saved as a template. This will ensure that all slides in the presentation are the same.

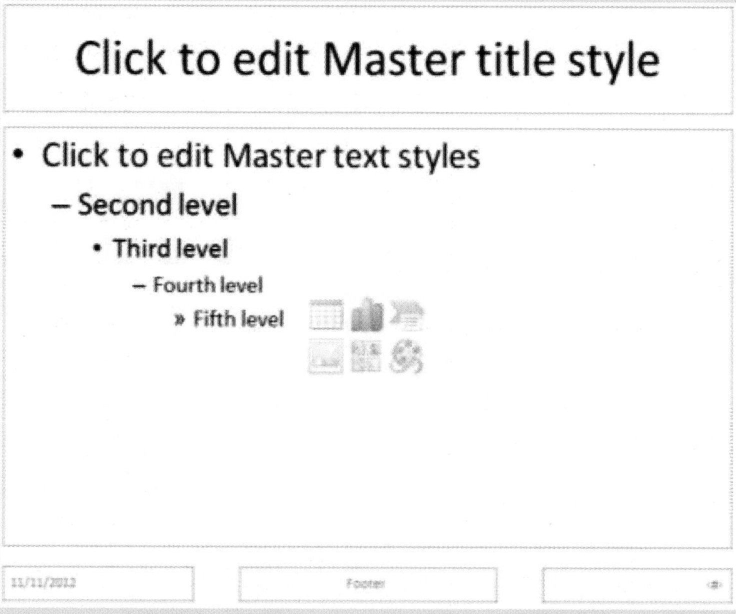


***Print presentation in slide and handout format***

It may be necessary to print a copy of the presentation for the presenter or the audience to refer to during the presentation (or for the audience to look at in their own time).

A presentation can be printed in slide format or in handout format.

Slide format will produce a copy of the presentation with one slide printed on one page. It is possible to print selected slides as well as the full presentation.

Handout format will produce a copy of the presentation with multiple slides on one page. The number of slides per page can be selected before printing. Depending on the number of slides chosen, space can be made available at the side for making notes.

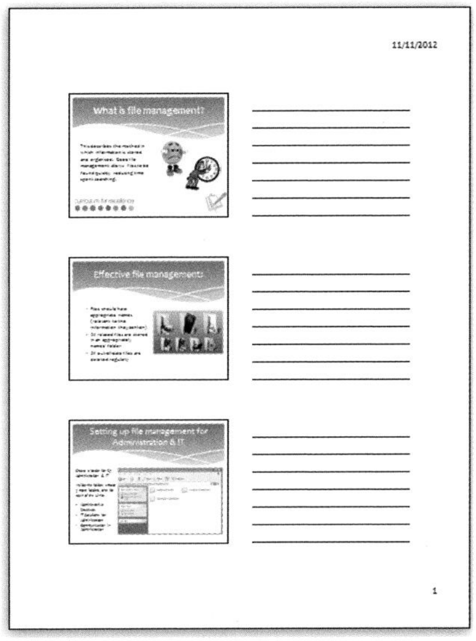


### *The slideshow*

To show the presentation to an audience you will need to connect the computer to a multimedia projector, which will display the presentation onto a large screen. Start the slideshow and move through the slides by pressing the mouse or an appropriate key on the keyboard, controlling the pace. A slideshow can be started from the beginning or a selected slide.

It is also possible to set up the presentation so that the slideshow will run automatically. Timings can be rehearsed so that each slide is left on screen for enough time for the audience to read the information.

## GO! Activity

Create a presentation that will introduce the Administration and IT course to new students.

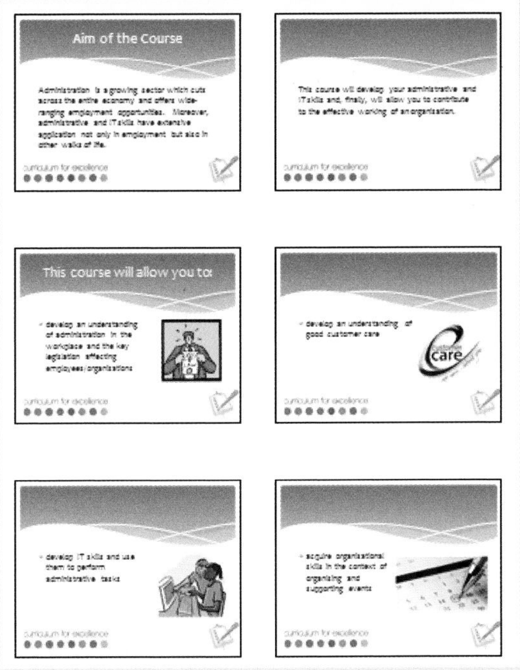


**Title slide:** Insert an appropriate title.

**Slide 1**: Aim of the course – Administration is a growing sector that cuts across the entire economy and offers wide-ranging employment opportunities. Moreover, administrative and IT skills have extensive applications, not only in employment but also in other walks of life.

**Slide 2**: This course will develop your administrative and IT skills and, finally, will allow you to contribute to the effective working of an organisation.

**Slide 3**: This course will allow you to develop an understanding of administration in the workplace and the key legislation affecting employees/organisations.

**Slide 4**: This course will allow you to develop an understanding of good customer care.

*(continued)*

**Slide 5**: This course will allow you to develop IT skills and use them to perform administrative tasks.

**Slide 6:** This course will allow you to acquire organisational skills in the context of organising and supporting events.

Include the following in your presentation:

- an appropriate title page
- a suitable background and colour/scheme and/or design template
- text formatting – font, size, style, alignment
- graphics (from clipart or the Internet)
- slide transitions
- text/object animation

Provide a printout of the presentation in an appropriate format.

**Watch point**

National 5 students may use the slide master.

## Questions

1. Give an example of when presentation software would be used.
2. Identify **two** advantages of using presentation software.
3. Other than a computer, suggest another item of equipment used to deliver a presentation to an audience.
4. Give **two** examples of how text can be formatted using presentation software.
5. Describe why a presentation should not include too many different types of animation on one slide.
6. Explain why action buttons would be included in a presentation.
7. State the benefit of using the slide master.

## Key questions

Prepare a presentation that could be used when providing induction training for new employees. The presentation should include information relating to the security of people, property and information.

1. Plan your presentation first – decide on the number of slides, the information to be included, where you might find appropriate graphics, etc.
2. Prepare your presentation using presentation software. Try to use as many different skills identified in the table on page 131 as you can.
3. Practise your presentation before presenting to the rest of the class.

## Skill

- Literacy
- Numeracy
- Employability
- Skills for learning, life and work

## Activity

1. Using a presentation that has already been created make sure that you know how to change from one view to another, e.g. from normal view to slide sorter. Practise re-ordering the slides.
2. Using a presentation that has already been created, practise adding action buttons to carry out the following:
   - **(a)** Move to the next slide
   - **(b)** Move to the previous slide
   - **(c)** Return to the first slide
   - **(d)** Go the last slide

## Summary

In this topic you have learned what is expected of you at both National 4 and National 5 levels, i.e. the skills you should be able to carry out at each level.

- You have learned who uses presentation software and why. Multimedia and presentation software can be used for delivering information to large audiences. For example, for training, in staff meetings, etc.
- You have learned the advantages of using presentation software – using graphics, sound and video in addition to text can help to make the presentation more interesting. The use of slide transition and animation can help to hold the audience's attention.
- You have learned what functions are available in presentation software to prepare and communicate simple information, for example formatting text, adding graphics, changing slide layout and adding animation.

## Learning Checklist

| | Skills, knowledge and understanding | Strength ☺ | 😐 | Weakness ☹ | Next steps |
|---|---|---|---|---|---|
| Functions | Insert, edit and format text | | | | • Refer to instructions<br>• Complete additional tasks<br>• Ask teacher for help |
| | Align text | | | | • Refer to instructions<br>• Complete additional tasks<br>• Ask teacher for help |
| | Insert graphics | | | | • Refer to instructions<br>• Complete additional tasks<br>• Ask teacher for help |
| | Use bullets | | | | • Refer to instructions<br>• Complete additional tasks<br>• Ask teacher for help |
| | Create chart(s) and/or table(s) | | | | • Refer to instructions<br>• Complete additional tasks<br>• Ask teacher for help |
| | Add and delete a slide | | | | • Refer to instructions<br>• Complete additional tasks<br>• Ask teacher for help |
| | Animate text/objects | | | | • Refer to instructions<br>• Complete additional tasks<br>• Ask teacher for help |
| | Import data from other applications/ Internet | | | | • Refer to instructions<br>• Complete additional tasks<br>• Ask teacher for help |
| | Change slide content layout | | | | • Refer to instructions<br>• Complete additional tasks<br>• Ask teacher for help |
| | Apply slide transitions | | | | • Refer to instructions<br>• Complete additional tasks<br>• Ask teacher for help |
| | Change slide order | | | | • Refer to instructions<br>• Complete additional tasks<br>• Ask teacher for help |
| | Apply and change background and colour scheme | | | | • Refer to instructions<br>• Complete additional tasks<br>• Ask teacher for help |
| | Insert footer objects | | | | • Refer to instructions<br>• Complete additional tasks<br>• Ask teacher for help |
| | Insert action buttons | | | | • Refer to instructions<br>• Complete additional tasks<br>• Ask teacher for help |
| | Use slide master | | | | • Refer to instructions<br>• Complete additional tasks<br>• Ask teacher for help |
| | Print presentation in slide and handout format | | | | • Refer to instructions<br>• Complete additional tasks<br>• Ask teacher for help |

# 12 Desktop publishing

**You should already know**

- I can approach familiar and new situations with confidence when selecting and using appropriate software to solve increasingly complex problems or issues. **TCH 4-03a**
- I can use ICT effectively in different learning contexts across the curriculum to access, select and present relevant information in a range of tasks. **TCH 4-03b**

**In this chapter you will learn about:**

- The use of desktop publishing software.
- The advantages of using desktop publishing software.
- How to use desktop publishing to produce a simple document.

## Using desktop publishing software

Desktop publishing (DTP) software allows you to look at the page of the document as a whole and to design the layout by marking areas for text and graphics. Text can be arranged in columns with large titles or headlines. Images can be imported from graphics packages, scanned or downloaded from the Internet.

All these features can be put together to produce newspapers, newsletters, pages for books, posters, brochures, leaflets, etc.

Most word processing packages have many of the features of desktop publishing packages but they are not as fast and it is more difficult to use them for complex layouts. Examples of desktop publishing software packages are Microsoft Publisher, Adobe InDesign and Quark Xpress.

### Advantages of using desktop publishing software

Desktop publishing and word processing are similar but there are a number of distinct advantages of using DTP. For example:

- There is more control over the way text is arranged and formatted.
- DTP can be used to bring lots of different files together on the same document.

You can import images into a DTP document from a scanner, graphics from a drawing package, frames from a video camera and text from a word processed document.

## Quick-look list

If you want to quickly check what you should be able to do using desktop publishing software, refer to the list shown below.

| Skill | Shown on page: |
|---|---|
| • Using templates | 143 |
| • Select and change font, font size | 143 |
| • Set and change margins | 143 |
| • Insert text, delete text, move text, format text | 143 |
| • Insert graphic | 143 |
| • Insert headers and footers | 143 |
| • Borders and shading | 143 |

## Functions of desktop publishing software

Many of the skills learned in word processing can also be used when working with DTP software.

***Using templates***

The use of templates will save time in the design stage of producing a document. Most desktop publishing packages will have a range of templates that the user can use. For example:

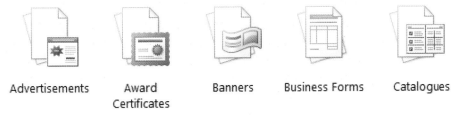

Advertisements  Award Certificates  Banners  Business Forms  Catalogues

The user can select the template of their choice and then simply edit the text/graphics. Templates can be customised by inserting company logos, addresses, and other items in the appropriate places.

***Formatting text/document***

Many of the functions of DTP software work in the same way as using word processing software.

- Text can be formatted by changing the font, size, style, alignment, etc.
- The document layout can be changed by altering margins.
- Borders and shading can be added.
- It is possible to rearrange the text within a document using the cut/copy and paste functions.
- Graphics can be added to produce a more professional-looking document.
- Headers and footers can be added.

Examples of documents that could be produced using desktop publishing software:

1. Poster template – includes text, graphics, etc. and can be customised to suit the individual/organisation

2. Newsletter template – includes text, columns, graphics, etc. and can be customised to suit the individual/organisation.

3. Envelope label template – includes text, graphics, etc. and can be customised to suit the individual/organisation

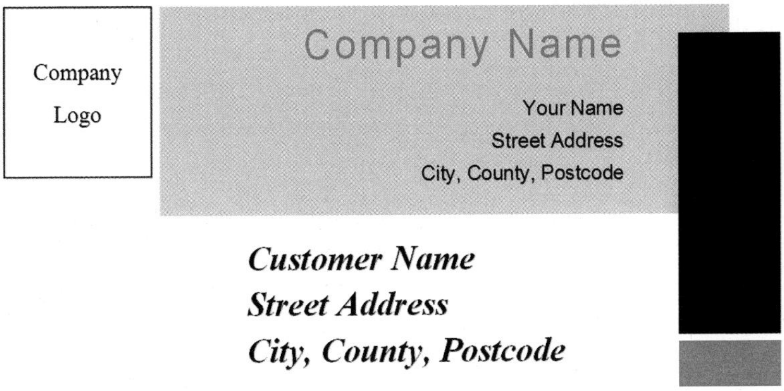


4. Certificate template – includes text, logo, etc. and can be customised to suit the individual/organisation

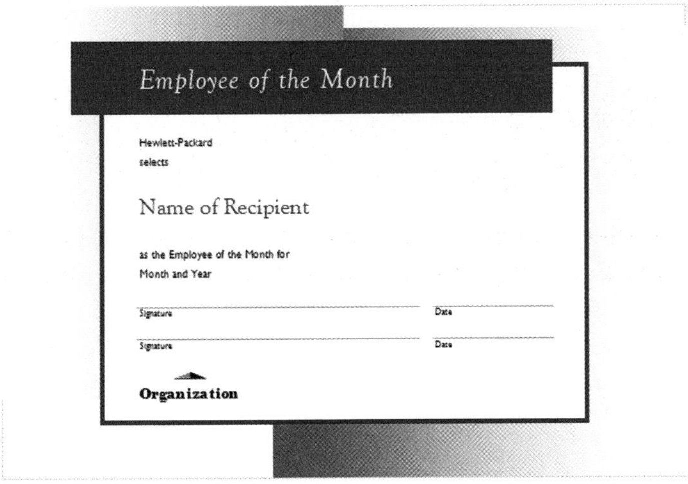


Desktop publishing software has been used in the production of this book.

> **Make the Link**
>
> You may be asked to produce a leaflet, newsletter or poster for other subjects. In Modern Studies you may be asked to design an election poster. In Business Management you may be asked to design a marketing leaflet for an organisation.

## GO! Activity

Use desktop publishing software to produce a school newsletter. The newsletter should use only one A4 sheet of paper once printed. You can design the newsletter yourself or use a template. Your newsletter should include the following:

- a main heading
- columns
- graphics
- appropriate margins
- different text formats, such as fonts, sizes and styles
- borders and shading where appropriate

## ? Questions

1. Give an example of where desktop publishing software could be used.
2. Describe **one** advantage of using desktop publishing software instead of word processing software.
3. Justify the use of a template when using desktop publishing software.
4. Give **three** examples of how text can be formatted using desktop publishing software.

### Watch point

Look at examples of newsletters produced within your own school. Include news like key dates, sporting events and celebrating successes.

### Skill

- Literacy
- Numeracy
- Employability
- Skills for learning, life and work

### Key questions

You have been asked to prepare documents to support a sporting event that has been organised within the school. The event will take place on the last Friday in June, from 1 pm to 3 pm. Medals will be awarded for gold, silver and bronze places. Use DTP software to complete the following tasks.

1. Prepare a leaflet that provides information on the sporting activities available during the event. Research and list **four** sporting activities in the leaflet and include text and some relevant graphics. The leaflet should also include a form to be used to sign up for the activities. Include spaces for the pupil's name, class, date of birth, chosen activities and for a parent/guardian signature.
2. Make a poster to advertise the event.
3. Prepare certificates for each of the four activities that can be completed with the winner's personal information after the event.

### GO! Activity

Use DTP software to produce the following for the school school (Christmas) music concert. This will take place on the second Friday in December at 7 pm. Tickets will cost £5 for adults and £3 for children or concessions.

1. Tickets
2. A poster
3. Invitations to be sent to local councillors

## Summary

In this topic you have learned what desktop publishing is and you can identify examples of what it can be used to produce.

- You have learned the advantages of using DTP software.
- You have learned what functions are available using DTP software and understand how to use these functions to produce a simple document that looks professional.

## Learning Checklist

| | Skills, knowledge and understanding | Strength ☺ | ☺ | Weakness ☹ | Next steps |
|---|---|---|---|---|---|
| Functions | Using templates | | | | • Refer to instructions<br>• Complete additional tasks<br>• Ask teacher for help |
| | Select and change font, font size | | | | • Refer to instructions<br>• Complete additional tasks<br>• Ask teacher for help |
| | Set and change margins | | | | • Refer to instructions<br>• Complete additional tasks<br>• Ask teacher for help |
| | Insert text, delete text, move text, format text | | | | • Refer to instructions<br>• Complete additional tasks<br>• Ask teacher for help |
| | Insert graphic | | | | • Refer to instructions<br>• Complete additional tasks<br>• Ask teacher for help |
| | Insert headers and footers | | | | • Refer to instructions<br>• Complete additional tasks<br>• Ask teacher for help |
| | Borders and shading | | | | • Refer to instructions<br>• Complete additional tasks<br>• Ask teacher for help |

# 13 Electronic methods of communication

**You should already know**

- Throughout all my learning, I can use search facilities of electronic sources to access and retrieve information, recognising the importance this has in my place of learning, at home and in the workplace. **TCH 2-01b**
- Pupils may have their own experience of using social media.

**In this chapter you will learn about:**

- Uses/advantages of e-mail.
- Disadvantages/problems associated with e-mail.
- Advantages of using an electronic diary.
- Different types of social media.

## Electronic mail (e-mail)

E-mail is information sent and received via computer. Text, graphics and files can all be sent instantly from one computer to another (if both users have an e-mail address).

### Uses and advantages of e-mail

- A fast method of sending (urgent) information. Messages can be sent instantly to anywhere in the world.
- A relatively inexpensive method of communication. It is cheaper than making a telephone call or posting a letter. E-mail can be sent, received, read and then deleted without using any paper.
- Attachments can be sent easily. Previously prepared files such as spreadsheets, database files, letters or pictures can be attached to the e-mail. This means that the person receiving the attachment has the option to print, edit and/or save the attached file to their computer. Sending a bulky document by e-mail is considerably cheaper than sending by post or courier.
- Group e-mail can be used. One e-mail can be prepared and sent to a number of different recipients at the same time. This ensures all recipients are sent the same information at the same time. Contact groups or distribution lists can be set up to include different people for different purposes.

- Messages can be flagged according to priority (high, low). This allows the recipient to prioritise the order in which he/she opens e-mail messages.
- A receipt/confirmation facility asks the recipient to let the sender know that they have received and opened the e-mail message they sent.
- Messages can be forwarded to other users. If someone receives a message they wish to let others see they can easily forward the e-mail to them.
- Copies (Cc) and blind copies (Bcc) of the e-mail can be sent to a number of people. If a Bcc is used the initial recipient will be unaware that Bcc-ed person has also received the e-mail.
- E-mail is convenient and allows communication at any time of the day. This is very useful for sending messages across different time zones. For example if an organisation wishes to communicate with an overseas branch the e-mail can be prepared and sent during the working day in one time zone and can be received and dealt with during the working day in another.
- Confidential information can be sent via e-mail as a password is usually required to access the e-mail accounts.
- Mailing lists can be created. Subscribers to a mailing list will receive e-mails containing relevant information on a regular basis – many businesses use this to send e-newsletters, announce any promotions etc.

## Disadvantages/problems of e-mail

- The sender needs to know the recipient's e-mail address (these are often long and complicated, which makes it difficult to remember them).
- Unless a sender requests a **read receipt** there is no way of knowing if the recipient has opened the e-mail.
- The account must be checked regularly.
- **Spam** and **junk** e-mail can clog up people's inboxes.
- **Viruses** can be easily spread via e-mail.
- Technical difficulties may arise that make it difficult to send/receive e-mail.

> **Watch point**
>
> You should never open an e-mail unless you know the sender.

**Watch point**

You should always think about who you are sending the e-mail to and compose it appropriately. A message to a customer or colleague should be more formal than a message to a friend– no text speak or emoticon/smileys should be used.

**Watch point**

You should try to use your e-mail account often, perhaps to send work to your teacher. Think of the savings you will make on printing costs and you are doing your bit for the environment!

## Using e-mail

In order to be able to use e-mail, an account must be set up. E-mail addresses usually follow the same format, for example: Username@companyname.co.uk

For the purpose of this course you should be able to:

1. Access your e-mail account and send a short message (you will need the recipient's e-mail address).
2. Receive an e-mail and reply to it using the reply function (this saves you keying in the recipient's e-mail address).
3. Identify e-mail messages that are urgent and mark them as high priority.

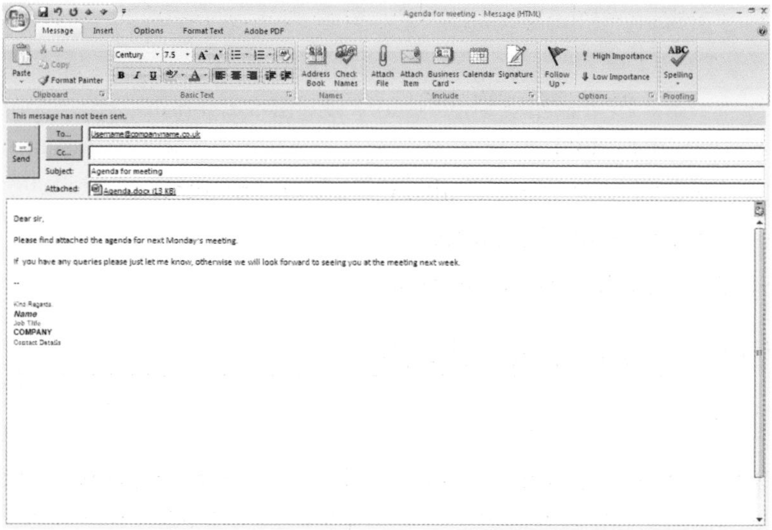


4. Create an address book of all the e-mail addresses you require. Using the address book saves time and effort when trying to remember different people's e-mail addresses (they are usually quite long and can be complicated).
5. Add an attachment.
6. Create a signature to make your e-mail look more personal.

## Electronic diary (e-diary)

An electronic diary is held on a computer. While it includes many features of a paper-based diary, such as storing appointments, personal details, to-do lists etc., it has many other features and advantages.

- Recurring meetings, for example weekly sales meetings, need only be entered once, this saves time writing (or keying in) the same information over and over.

- Alerts can be used to remind the user about an appointment.
- The diaries of several people may be linked and can be checked to find a suitable date/time for a meeting.
- Double-booking of appointments is highlighted, bringing this to the attention of the user.
- Some electronic diaries will link to an e-mail facility and any changes made to appointments will be e-mailed to relevant people.

For the purpose of this course you should be able to:

1. Access an e-diary.
2. Enter an appointment – date, time, duration and location of meeting.
3. Enter a recurring meeting.
4. Set a reminder.
5. Print the calendar in daily, weekly and monthly view.
6. Create a to-do list (task).
7. Access other users calendars.

## Emerging technologies

### Blogs

Blogs are set up on the Internet by individuals who wish to communicate their thoughts and opinions on a particular topic; there are blogs on virtually anything you can think of – photography, business education, recipes, personal diaries, hobbies etc. Blogs can bring people from around the world who share similar interests together to share ideas, make friends and even do business together.

### Discussion group and forums

A discussion group is an online forum for individuals to discuss topics of interest. Posters add their comment, which others can read and then respond to. It is an informal and voluntary way to exchange ideas and information and keeps people up-to-date on topics of interest.

### Instant messaging

Instant messaging (IM) is a way of communicating in real time (instantly). You can send IMs to anyone who is online at the same time, and you can reply immediately to messages sent to you, and so on. Two or more people can join in a 'conversation' at the same time. IMs can be used to have a quick conversation between colleagues working on the same project in different areas of the office. Instant messaging is not a secure method of communication.

### Podcasts and vodcasts

Podcasting/vodcasting is an audio/video file which can be downloaded to a computer or mobile device (such as a smartphone or tablet). It means that people can listen or watch at a time that is convenient to them.

### Websites

Many organisations will have their own website. They will use this to communicate with customers – promoting their products with pictures, product details (size, colour etc.) and customer reviews – to encourage people to buy the product or service. Many organisations have an e-commerce facility on their website, which allows customers to purchase products online. Organisations will also use their website to keep (potential) customers informed of special offers etc.

### Social media

Social media is a way of talking to other people via your computer, allowing you to exchange pictures, information, ideas, opinions etc. Social media is becoming more popular with businesses as a way to communicate with customers and potential customers.

- Twitter is an information network that connects people to the latest stories, ideas, opinions and news. Individuals choose to 'follow' whoever interests them, whether this is

**Watch point**

Technology develops rapidly. The emerging technologies mentioned here are current as this book goes to print. However, there may now be more current, relevant technology that you could use – try to keep up-to-date with developments.

an individual, business, news outlet etc. Businesses can use Twitter to quickly share information about their products and services. It also allows a 'conversation' between the follower and the business about a product/ service, which can then be 'retweeted' to many more potential customers.

- Facebook, Bebo and MySpace are social networking services that let you connect with friends, co-workers, and others who share similar interests or who have common backgrounds. Businesses use these services as it gives them direct access to customers and potential customers.
- LinkedIn is a business version of Facebook – it connects individuals with people they know on a professional basis. It allows the user to see other people's business contacts and to ask for introductions in order to do business with them.
- Virtual learning environments (VLEs) use the Internet to allow remote access to learning materials, for example notes, tasks, homework, tests etc. Students can either work through the materials at their own pace before submitting to the 'teacher' for checking and tracking, or they can participate while a teacher conducts a live class – communicating through a microphone, chat rights, or by writing on the 'board'. Edmodo is a VLE that you may have used in school.

**Watch point**

Try and find out what courses you could study using a VLE. You can stay in Scotland and listen to lectures from anywhere in the world!

For the purpose of this course you should be able to use emerging technologies such as:

- blogs
- podcasts
- websites
- social media
- VLEs

## Method

When communicating with customers, clients and employees it is important that the correct method of communication is used:

- Is it appropriate? Will all intended recipients receive the information?
- Is it the most cost effective?
- How quickly is the information required?

This table shows some examples of how information could be communicated using electronic communication.

**Watch point**

Always ensure the message being conveyed is appropriate in terms of context, audience and purpose.

| Information | Appropriate method of electronic communication |
|---|---|
| Announcement of special offers to customers/ potential customers. | • E-mail (subscribers to mailing list)<br>• Social media<br>• Website |
| Colleagues communicating in different areas of the organisation. | • E-mail<br>• Instant messaging |
| Information on products – details, pictures etc. | • Website |
| Confirmation of a hotel booking. | • E-mail |
| Information to all employees working in the Sales Department. | • E-mail – contact group/distribution list |
| Employee database file required by Human Resources department immediately. | • E-mail with attachment |
| Meeting scheduled for next week with all heads of departments. | • Electronic diary |
| Feedback from customers. | • Social media<br>• Blogs<br>• Discussion groups |

## Activity

Go to www.bbc.co.uk/webwise and select 'E-mail and sharing' then 'Sending e-mail'.

1. Select 'Step-by-step lesson on using e-mail'.
2. Work your way through each of the lessons.
   (a) Introduction
   (b) What is e-mail
   (c) Sending and receiving e-mail
   (d) Composing an e-mail
   (e) Address book
   (f) Practice
3. For additional practice you could try Courses→ Internet basics→E-mail with Dick and Harry.

## Make the link

- You could use a VLE to help you practise and revise subjects such as Maths.
- You may already have access to a blog created by a teacher in another subject such as Business Management.
- In Administration and IT (National 4) when completing the Added Value Unit you will be expected to make use of appropriate technologies where necessary and communicate using electronic methods (showing a basic awareness of the communication's context, audience and purpose).

## ? Questions

1. List **three** advantages of using e-mail.
2. State three problems of relying on e-mail.
3. Describe three advantages of using an electronic diary.
4. Explain what a podcast is.
5. Give a description of instant messaging.
6. Describe how instant messaging could be used in a business.
7. Explain a business use of each of the following:
   (a) Twitter
   (b) Facebook/Bebo/MySpace
   (c) LinkedIn
8. Complete the following table with the most appropriate method of electronic communication.

| Information | Appropriate method of electronic communication |
|---|---|
| Announcement of special offers to customers/potential customers | |
| Information on products – details, pictures etc. | |
| Information to all employees working in the Sales Department | |
| Meeting scheduled for next week with all heads of departments | |
| Feedback from customers | |

## Skill

- Decision-making
- ICT
- Research
- Literacy
- Employability
- Skills for learning, life and work

## Key questions

1. Antony Taylor, Managing Director of Bootlocker UK, wishes to organise a whole-staff meeting at the Glasgow branch of the organisation.
   **(a)** Outline **one** feature of e-mail that would be useful when organising this event.
   **(b)** Name **one** other method of electronic communication that could be used when organising this event.
   **(c)** Describe **one** feature of the method mentioned in (b) that would be useful when organising this event.
2. Suggest **two** benefits to an organisation of communicating by e-mail.
3. Describe **two** disadvantages of using e-mail.
4. Justify the replacement by an organisation of its paper diaries with an electronic version.
5. Describe **one** feature of a discussion group.
6. Outline **one** advantage of using instant messaging.

## Activity

***Individually or in pairs***

1. Select a topic from National 4 or National 5 Administration and IT that you wish to revise. Make a podcast, using your notes, which you can download and listen to as you walk to school.
2. Access your electronic diary and create your timetable for next week. You should also include any after-school activities that you attend. Use the to-do list section (or tasks section) to list any coursework or homework deadlines you may have.
3. There are many VLEs available online, for example, www.khanacademy.org. Access this website and use it to revise a topic of your choice (it does not need to be from Administration and IT).

***Group or whole class***

1. Set up a contacts group/distribution list using the e-mail addresses of pupils in your Administration and IT class.

2. Think of all the topics covered within the Administration and IT course. Each student should select a topic and prepare a set of summary/revision notes.
3. To ensure the summary/revision notes contain all the required information use peer assessment: each student should proofread another students's work. Check for content and accuracy as well as spelling, grammar etc.
4. E-mail the revision notes as an attachment to each student in the class using the contacts group previously set up in 1. You should end up with a full set of summary notes that could be used when revising for the final exam!
5. Create a class blog! It could contain:
   - information on the subject
   - notes
   - tasks
   - homework
   - dates for diary etc.

You must remember to update it on a regular basis!

## Summary

There are many reasons why businesses use e-mail. The advantages include: sending attachments; using e-mail groups; showing priority of messages being sent; the receipt/ confirmation facility; forwarding the same message to another person including Cc and Bcc; and the creation of mailing lists. It is convenient, printing costs can be avoided and confidential information can be sent.

However, we should remember that there are some disadvantages/problems associated with e-mail, such as: the sender needs to know the e-mail address of the recipient; there is often no way of knowing if the recipient has read the information contained in the e-mail; it requires regular checking; spam/junk e-mail can be a nuisance; and viruses can be spread via e-mail.

An electronic diary is similar to a paper-based diary, in that it stores appointments etc. However, there are many advantages to using an electronic diary, such as: recurring meetings need only be keyed in once (saving time); alerts can be used; the diaries of several people can be linked; double-booking can be brought to the attention of the user; any changes made to appointments can be automatically e-mailed to the relevant people.

Technology advances very quickly and businesses must keep up if they are to remain competitive. Blogs, discussion groups, instant messaging, websites and social media are all methods businesses can use to keep in touch with customers/clients/employees etc.

Organisations should be aware of the different methods of communicating with customers/ clients and employees and ensure they use the most appropriate.

## Learning Checklist

| | Skills, knowledge and understanding | Strength ☺ | ☺ | Weakness ☹ | Next steps |
|---|---|---|---|---|---|
| Functions | **1.** I understand the uses/advantages of e-mail | | | | |
| | **2.** I understand the disadvantages/problems associated with e-mail | | | | |
| | **3.** I understand the advantages of using an electronic diary | | | | |
| | **4.** I understand different types of social media | | | | |

# Answers

## Chapter 1

### *Questions*

1. Job description
2. A job description provides information that allows the job applicant to decide if the job is right for them and if they would like to undertake the tasks described.
3. Job description – tasks and duties to be undertaken by the person appointed. Person specification – qualities and skills required by the person appointed.
4. Word processing business documents; using databases and spreadsheets; using technology to prepare and communicate information; organising events; answering the telephone; working in reception; using the photocopier and fax machine; sending and receiving e-mails; making diary appointments; using internet and emerging technologies.
5. Job title, salary, working conditions etc.
6. Areas of strength and areas that need further development.
7. To identify training requirements of employees. To help further develop the employee's career, for example promotion.

### *Key questions*

1. Duties: any two from the following: using databases and spreadsheets; using technology to prepare and communicate information; organising events; working in reception; using the photocopier and fax machine; sending and receiving e-mails; making diary appointments; using the Internet and emerging technologies.

   Qualities/skills: any three from the following: ability to accurately key in data; ability to create and edit word-processed documents, spreadsheets, databases; confident at using e-mail; ability to organise events; ability to follow verbal and written instructions; motivated; keen; dependable; reliable etc.
2. (a) Job description and person specification.

   (b) Job description – any relevant tasks; person specification – any relevant skills/qualities (see 1. for more details)

(c) Job description – to decide if the job is right for them (if they would like to do the tasks etc.); person specification – to decide if they have the necessary skills, qualifications, etc. to be able to do the job

## Chapter 2

### *Questions*

1. A mission statement gives an outline of the main intentions of an organisation. It sets out the organisation's aims and objectives.
2. It is used to tell external customers about the organisation and its ideals. It is also used to give employees an idea/vision of what the organisation hopes to achieve and helps them to focus their work towards achieving this goal.
3. The organisation can rely on a group of customers who will always buy their product/service rather than use another organisation. Loyal customers may also encourage others to become customers.
4. Any two of the following:
   - **Satisfied customers** – if customers are happy with the products/services being provided they will return and recommend the organisation to others.
   - **Keeping loyal customers** – this can be done by offering customers loyalty schemes, for example Boots Advantage Card, Nectar Points.
   - **Attracting new customers** – this might be as a result of a recommendation from an existing customer or persuasion through loyalty schemes/advertising.
   - **Satisfied and motivated employees** – a clear customer-care strategy allows employees to deal with all customers effectively, reducing stress.
   - **Lower staff turnover** – employees are not stressed and will stay with the organisation.
   - **Reduced costs** – the cost of recruiting new employees is not necessary.
   - **Good/improved reputation** – recommendations from existing customers will improve the image of the organisation, if a customer has had a good experience with an organisation, they are likely to talk about it.
   - **Competitive edge** – a good reputation/more effective performance will mean that customers are more likely to choose that organisation rather than a competitor.

- **Increased sales/profits** – more customers (loyal and new) will mean that the organisation will increase the value of their sales and therefore increase their profit.

5. Any of the following:
   - **Dissatisfied customers** – if customers are unhappy about the products/services being provided, they will not return and will tell others of their dissatisfaction.
   - **Loss of customers** – dissatisfied customers will look for products/services elsewhere.
   - **Bad publicity** – dissatisfied customers will talk!
   - **Demotivated employees** – employees who do not receive appropriate customer care training, or have not been advised of the organisation's customer care strategy, may make mistakes or not deal with customers effectively, leading to stress.
   - **High staff turnover** – unhappy employees will leave to work elsewhere.
   - **Increased costs** – the costs of recruiting/training new staff will be high.
   - **Poor reputation** – the organisation will gain a poor reputation through bad publicity and customers/employees talking about their dissatisfaction/demotivation.
   - **Poor competitive edge** – customers will be more likely to choose a competitor as they are performing more effectively.
   - **Decreased sales/profits** – fewer customers (the loss of loyal customers and not attracting new customers) will result in lower sales and therefore lower profits.
   - **Legal action** – employees not complying with consumer legislation may lead to customers taking legal action.

*Key questions*

1. Another employee, for example the receptionist.
2. Anyone who buys the organisation's product/service.
3. A customer service policy is a written statement of the organisation's policy and their plans for dealing with their customers.
4. Customer satisfaction can be monitored by (any two of the following):
   - Surveying their customers' opinions (this could be done online, by phone or by post).

- Using a mystery shopper to measure satisfaction.
- Analysing loyalty card use (frequency, types of products).

**5.** A mission statement is used to give employees an idea/vision of what the organisation hopes to achieve and helps them to focus their work towards achieving this goal.

**6.** Putting the customer first; communicating with customers effectively, ensuring that staff are knowledgeable about products/services; providing a good after sales service; dealing with complaints effectively.

**7.** Increased sales/profits will result from any of the benefits of good customer service. For example, attracting new customers will lead to an increase in sales and therefore profits.

**8.** Any three of the following:

- **Dissatisfied customers** – if customers are unhappy about the products/services being provided, they will not return and will tell others of their dissatisfaction.
- **Loss of customers** – dissatisfied customers will look for products/services elsewhere.
- **Bad publicity** – dissatisfied customers will talk!
- **Demotivated employees** – employees who do not receive appropriate customer care training, or have not been advised of the organisation's customer care strategy may make mistakes, not deal with customers effectively, leading to stress.
- **High staff turnover** – unhappy employees will leave to work elsewhere.
- **Increased costs** – the costs of recruiting/training new staff will be high.
- **Poor reputation** – the organisation will gain a poor reputation through bad publicity and customers/employees talking of their dissatisfaction/demotivation.
- **Poor competitive edge** – customers will be more likely to choose a competitor as they are performing more effectively.
- **Decreased sales/profits** – fewer customers (the loss of loyal customers and not attracting new customers) will result in lower sales and therefore lower profits.
- **Legal action** – employees not complying with consumer legislation may lead to customers taking legal action.

## Chapter 3

*Questions*

1. Position desks to avoid trailing cables or use a cable management system; position filing cabinets away from the door; never store heavy materials in a hard-to-reach place (provide a step ladder if required); mop up any liquids that have been spilled (use a danger sign if the floor is still wet); keep passageways free from obstacles.
2. Accident report form; accident book.
3. To allow employees to access the form, complete it on the computer and e-mail it immediately to the relevant person.
4. The HSE work with local authorities to check the standards of health, safety and welfare of organisations as well as giving advice on how to prevent people being made ill or injured at work.
5. The name of the person(s) responsible for carrying out health and safety checks within the organisation – and how often this will occur; appropriate health and safety training to be given to employees; the organisation's evacuation procedure; how often employees will be consulted on day-to-day health and safety conditions; details on maintenance of equipment.
6. Training given to new employees to introduce them to the organisation.
7.

| Responsibilities of Employee | Responsibilities of Organisation |
|---|---|
| Take reasonable care of their own health and safety and the health and safety of others. | Ensure safe methods of working. |
| Cooperate with the employer on health and safety matters. | Ensure safe working conditions. |
| Not misuse or interfere with anything provided for employees' health and safety. | Ensure all employees receive information and training on health and safety. |
| | Ensure that equipment is safe and properly maintained. |
| | Provide protective clothing where necessary. |

8. Employee – making use of adjustment facilities for the VDU; adjusting chair for maximum comfort; arranging desk and screen to avoid glare. Organisation – assess workstation requirement; provide adjustable seating; provide adjustable and tilting screens; provide health and safety training for

employees; organise daily work of VDU users so that they take regular rest breaks or changes in activity.

9. Provide a well-stocked first aid box; appoint a first aider; inform staff of first-aid procedures; keep a record of all accidents/incidents.
10. Assess fire risks in the organisation; provide appropriate fire-fighting equipment; check and maintain fire-fighting equipment; provide warning systems; train employees in fire procedures; regularly check evacuation procedures.

### *Key questions*

1. (a) Two from: trailing cables; opened filing cabinet; person standing on a chair to reach high shelves; fire exit blocked.

   (b) Two from: chair which is not adjustable; glare on computer screen from window with no blinds; pain in wrist caused by repetitive strain injury.
2. Take reasonable care of their own health and safety and the health and safety of others; cooperate with the employer on health and safety matters; not misuse or interfere with anything provided for employees' health and safety.
3. (a) Health and Safety (First Aid) Regulations 1981; Fire Precautions (Places of Work) Regulations 1995.

   (b) Health and Safety (First Aid) Regulations 1981 – provide a well-stocked first aid box; appoint a first aider; inform staff of first aid procedures; keep a record of all accidents/incidents.

   Fire Precautions (Places of Work) Regulations 1995 – assess fire risks in the organisation; provide appropriate fire-fighting equipment such as fire extinguishers; check and maintain fire-fighting equipment; provide warning systems (and check them regularly); train employees in fire procedures; regularly check evacuation procedures (regular fire drills would help check routes are appropriate, timings are acceptable, etc.)

## Chapter 4

### *Questions*

1. It is usually located at the entrance of the organisation and is usually the first place visitors will see.
2. Three from: staff ID badges/security passes should be shown to the receptionist each time they wish to gain entry to the building; monitoring CCTV – areas within and out with the building can be observed and recorded; controlling intercom/entryphone/buzzer system – anyone wishing to enter the

building must first contact the receptionist who will check their identity before the door is opened; keeping appointments book, visitors' book, staff in/out book to record information on who has been in the building at specific times; issuing visitors' badges – these allow authorised visitors to be identified by staff.

3. Access is restricted to those who are authorised and who have the appropriate number/card. Swipe cards can be programmed to allow an employee access to certain areas that they have permission to be in and not others. Similarly, staff may hold the keypad/combination number for only the areas they require access to and not others.

4. Three from: attach equipment to desk – computer keyboards/monitors etc could be bolted to desks; mark equipment with UV (ultra violet) pens – in the event of property being stolen police would be able to quickly find out the owner of the property; keep an inventory of equipment – keeping a record of equipment means that it any equipment goes missing it will quickly be noticed; security cables – may be used with portable laptops/notebooks/netbooks, a steel cable secures the item to any solid or fixed object; ensure office doors and windows are locked before leaving the premises; alarm – this may be set at night when the building is empty; security guard – a security guard may patrol the premises (usually at night) to protect the building; security lighting could also be used at night to detect motion; security blinds – strong shutters can be placed over doors and windows to prevent burglary, theft and vandalism.

5. The **computer** can only be used when the username/password is entered correctly. **Files** - each username and password will give the user access to the information they require, i.e. access rights.

6. Saving files as read-only documents; ensuring storage media is labelled and stored in a locked drawer; inserting security ID cards/keys into the computer; using voiceprint/fingerprint recognition or iris/signature scanners; installing anti-virus software; using encryption software.

7. Taking a second copy of the data, which is then stored separately.

8. The Act states that personal data must be: fairly and lawfully processed; used for the registered purpose only; adequate, relevant and not excessive; accurate; kept for no longer than is necessary; kept securely; processed in line with the individual's legal rights; transferred to countries outside the European Economic Area, only if the individual's rights can be assured.

9. To prohibit unlawful access to computer systems.

## Chapter 5

### *Questions*

1. Internet browser.
2. Access the electronic diaries of all those attending to identify a suitable date/time.
3. Any three of the following:
   - graphics can be inserted
   - change of font/size/style/colour
   - borders/shading can be used
   - Word Art can be inserted
4. A notice of meeting and agenda can be created using WP/DTP software. These can then be posted or can be sent as an e-mail attachment (to a group).
5. Costs can be analysed using spreadsheet software.
6. Set a reminder using an electronic diary.

Use a house style booklet to ensure all documents are keyed in to the same standard; use the spell check facility to ensure that there are no spelling mistakes; proofread all documents to reduce errors.

7. Any two of the following:
   - Thank you letters
   - Minutes of Meeting
   - Attendance register
   - Evaluation forms

## Chapter 7

### *Questions*

1. Column – the space between two vertical lines that run up and down a spreadsheet table; row – the space between two horizontal lines that run across a spreadsheet table; cell – the space in the spreadsheet table where the column and row meet.
2. Text, numbers, formulae.
3. One from: different font, size, style, alignment, borders/shading.
4. Two from: formatted as currency, percentage, date, decimal places.

**5.** (a) Any two of the following:

- Sales
- Purchases
- Finance
- Human Resources

(b) Any task from:

- Sales
  - Calculate sales figures.
  - Create charts/graphs to help analyse sales figures.
  - Prepare 'What if?' scenarios, e.g. 'What would be the effect on a company's profit if we reduced pricesby 4%?'
- Purchases
  - Record issue and receipt of stock.
  - Complete order forms.
- Finance
  - Calculate employee wages.
  - Calculate the profit/loss of the organisation.
  - Prepare departmental budgets.
- Human Resources
  - Record employees' absences/holidays.
  - Calculate training costs.

**6.** Any two of the following:

- Present your data effectively by using formatting features.
- Calculate and recalculate quickly and accurately using formulae.
- Replicate formulae saving time, reducing errors.
- Sort data.
- Carry out 'What if?' scenarios.
- Display data graphically.

**7.** To copy the contents of one cell into others (this can include a calculation)

**8.** (a) COUNT

(b) MINIMUM

(c) SUM

### *Key questions*

1. Students should use word processing software to produce a report. Possible text to be included in the report is shown below.

   - Purpose of a spreadsheet:
     - A powerful tool for carrying out calculations and testing different mathematical possibilities.
     - Calculations can be carried out using formulae/ functions.
     - Graphs can charts can be created.
     - 'What if' scenarios can be created.
   - Examples of tasks carried out using spreadsheets:
     - Record employees' absences/holidays.
     - Calculate training costs.
     - Calculate employee wages.
     - Calculate the profit/loss of the organisation.
     - Prepare departmental budgets.
     - Calculate sales figures.
     - Create charts/graphs to help analyse sales figures.
     - Prepare 'what if?' scenarios, for example 'what would be the effect on a company's profit if we reduced prices by 4%?'
     - Record issue and receipt of stock.
     - Complete order forms.
   - Advantages of using spreadsheets:
     - present your data effectively by using formatting features.
     - calculate and recalculate quickly and accurately using formulae.
     - replicate formulae saving time, reducing errors.
     - sort data.
     - carry out 'what if?' scenarios.
     - display data graphically.

## Chapter 8

### *Questions*

1. File – a collection of records; record – a collection of fields (about one person/thing); field – single piece of information (about one person/thing).
2. Relational database.
3. (a) Add a new record; (b) delete the fax field.
4. Text, number, date/time, currency, yes/no.
5. (a) Human Resources, Sales, Purchases. (b) Human Resources – store employee details; Sales – store customer details; Purchases Department – store supplier details.
6. Any two of the following:
   - Records can be found quickly using the **search** facility.
   - Records can arranged into the required order quickly using the **sort** facility.
   - A **query** can be used to create a **report**.
   - The **mailmerge** facility can be used to create personalised letters.

### *Key questions*

1. Students should use presentation software to prepare a presentation. Possible text to be included in the presentation is shown below
   - Purpose of a database
     - A database is a collection of related information.
     - A database allows us to search for information very quickly and allows us to sort the information easily.
     - The required data can be then be presented in the form of a printed report.
   - Examples of tasks carried out using databases:
     - Store employee details.
     - Store customer details.
     - Store supplier details.
   - Advantages of using databases:
     - Records can be found quickly using the **search** facility.
     - Records can arranged into the required order quickly using the **sort** facility.
     - A **query** can be used to create a **report**.

- The **mailmerge** facility can be used to create personalised letters.

## Chapter 10

### *Questions*

1. Travel/accommodation information; latest travel advice; travel routes; latest travel information; competitors' prices/promotions; potential supplier's deals; latest news.
2. **Web browser** – a software application used to access, retrieve and view information on the Internet.

   **Search engine** – keywords are typed in and a list of relevant websites is found (used when unsure of website address).

   **Search box** – allows the user to type in keywords to find relevant information contained within the website.

   **Hyperlink** – allow the user to go from one part of the website to another when clicked on.

   **Download** – information from a website copied on to an individual's computer.

   **Bookmarks/Favourites** – allow the user to store the addresses of frequently visited websites.
3. Information is usually up-to-date; a vast range of information is available; websites may give more detailed information than brochures or catalogues; convenience; information is instantly available.
4. Information on the Internet may be inaccurate and therefore unreliable.
5. Check the website is reputable/from a well-known organisation; ensure the website is updated on a regular basis; look carefully at the website to ensure it is well designed; use a secure website.
6. Out-of-date information could result in missing out on sales/orders for the organisation; reports may include inaccuracies and bias; personal details may be hacked and bank accounts etc accessed.
7. An intranet is an internal network used to share information *within* the organisation.
8. Three from: access company information; internal e-mail; electronic diary facilities; sharing software; all employees have access to the same current information; time is saved as information needs only to be updated once; cost savings as all information is stored electronically reducing paper and

photocopying costs; communication (particularly in large organisations) is improved through use of internal e-mail, electronic diaries etc

***Key questions***

(Sample answer)

Travel

| Train | | |
|---|---|---|
| Sunday (date) | Depart Inverness | 0940 hours |
| | Arrive Stirling | 1234 hours |
| | Depart Stirling | 1325 hours |
| | Arrive Glasgow Queen Street | 1405 hours |
| Thursday (date) | Depart Glasgow Queen Street | 0710 hours |
| | Arrive Inverness | 1026 hours |

| Flights | | |
|---|---|---|
| Monday | Depart Glasgow | 1350 hours |
| | Arrive Paris | 1820 hours |
| Wednesday | Depart Paris | 1905 hours |
| | Arrive Glasgow | 2145 hours |

Please note:

- If changeover then connection times must be shown.
- Travel by bus is also acceptable.

| Accommodation | |
|---|---|
| Glasgow | Grand Central Hotel, 96 Gordon Street, Glasgow, G1 3SF |
| Paris | Hotel du Louvre, Louvre-Place Vendome, Paris |

## Chapter 11

***Questions***

1. Presentations are used when passing on information to an audience. For example, the Training Officer may deliver induction training to new employees, the Sales Manager

may deliver a presentation on the sales targets to Sales Representatives, etc.

2. Any two of the following:
   - Information can be formatted to emphasise important information.
   - Presentation can be delivered at a pace to suit the audience, allowing for discussion to take place.
   - Slides can be created/edited very quickly for a different audience.
   - Information from other applications can also be included in the presentation (graphs/charts created in a spreadsheet package).
   - Printed handouts can accompany a presentation (so that the audience can refer back to in their own time).
3. Multimedia/data projector, screen, interactive whiteboard.
4. Font/size/style.
5. Can be distracting for the audience.
6. Action buttons are built-in button shapes that the user can add to the presentation, and then make an action occur when the mouse is clicked or when someone moves the mouse over the button. For example, to move to the next slide, move to the previous slide, return the first slide, etc.
7. Master slides are used to set the layout and standard formatting on **all** slides in the presentation. The placeholders (e.g. the title box), objects and formatting (font size, style, etc.) on the master slides are automatically applied to every slide in the presentation.

## Chapter 12

*Questions*

1. To produce newspapers, newsletters, pages for books, posters, brochures, leaflets, etc.
2. Any one of the following:
   - There is more control over the way is arranged and formatted.
   - Desktop publishing can be used to bring lots of different file together on the same document.
3. To save time in the design stage of producing a document.
4. Font, size, style, alignment.

## Chapter 13

### *Questions*

1. Three from: attachments can be sent; group e-mail can be used; priority of messages can be shown; a receipt/ confirmation facility can be used; messages can be forwarded to other users; copies and blind copies can be sent to a number of people; convenient; confidential information can be password-protected; mailing lists can be created; printing may be avoided – cost savings.
2. Three from: technical difficulties may arise; requires regular checking; unless a send requests a 'read receipt' there is no way of knowing if the recipient has opened the e-mail.
3. Three from: recurring meetings, e.g. weekly sales meetings need only be entered once; alerts can be used to remind the user of an appointment; diaries of several people may be linked and can be checked to find a suitable date/time for a meeting; double-booking of appointments is highlighted, bringing it to the attention of the user; some electronic diaries will link to an e-mail facility and any changes made to appointments will be e-mailed to relevant people.
4. An audio file that can be downloaded to a computer or mobile device (such as a smartphone, tablet etc).
5. A way of communicating in real time i.e. instantly.
6. To have a quick conversation between colleagues working on the same project in different areas of the office.
7. (a) Twitter – to quickly share information about their products and services.

   (b) Facebook/Bebo/MySpace – it gives them direct access to customers and potential customers.

   (c) LinkedIn – It allows the user to see other individual's contacts and to ask their contact to introduce them to others in order to do business with them.
8.

| Information | Appropriate method of electronic communication |
|---|---|
| Announcement of special offers to customers/ potential customers. | E-mail<br>Social media<br>Website |

| Information | Appropriate method of electronic communication |
|---|---|
| Information on products – details, pictures etc. | Website |
| Information to all employees working in the Sales Department. | E-mail – contact group/distribution list |
| Meeting scheduled for next week with all heads of departments. | Electronic diary |
| Feedback from customers. | Social media |

*Key questions*

1. (a) Distribution list/contact group – one e-mail can be prepared and sent to a number of recipients at the same time.

   (b) Electronic diary.

   (c) Diaries of several people may be linked and can be checked to find a suitable date/time for a meeting.

2. Two from: attachments can be sent; group e-mail can be used; priority of messages can be shown; printing can be avoided; fast method of sending (urgent) information; relatively inexpensive.

3. Three from: sender needs to know recipient's e-mail address; unless a 'read receipt' is requested there is no way of knowing if the recipient has opened the e-mail; requires regular checking; spam e-mail/junk e-mail can be received; viruses can be easily spread via e-mail; technical difficulties may arise.

4. Recurring meetings need only be keyed in once; alerts can be used; diaries of several people may be linked and can be checked to find a suitable date/time for a meeting; double-booking of appointments is highlighted; some electronic diaries will link to an e-mail facility and any changes made to the appointments will be e-mailed to relevant people.

5. One from: a discussion group is an online forum for individuals to discuss topics of interest; people add their comments that others can read and then respond to; it is an informal and voluntary way to exchange ideas and information and keeps people up-to-date on topics of interest.

6. You will see the message being sent by an individual and you can reply immediately.